STEP BY STEP ART SCHOOL

AIRBRUSHING

JACK BUCHAN

HAMLYN

SPORTS EDITIONS LIMITED

Managing Director	Richard Dewing
Creative Director	Mary Hamlyn
Art Director	Rob Kelland
Senior Designer	Sandra Cowell
Design Assistant	Lyndon Brooks
Editor	Tom Whiting

This edition published in 1991 by
Paul Hamlyn Publishing
part of Reed International Books Ltd,
Michelin House, 81 Fulham Road,
London SW3 6RB

ISBN 0 600 57441 5

Designed and edited by
Sports Editions Limited
3 Greenlea Park
Prince George's Road
London SW19 2JD

Layout by Millions Design
Origination by J. Film in Bangkok
Printed in Hong Kong

Credits

pp8-9, Alberto Vargas, © Astrid V Conte and Max Vargas (VARGAS is a registered trademark owned exclusively by Vargas, a California Partnership, USA); p10, Mary Lynn; p11, The Robert Opie Collection; p12 (top and bottom), © London Transport Museum; p13, Nouvelles Images, © Henry Mouron; p14, Alberto Vargas, © Astrid V Conte and Max Vargas; p15 (left and right), Trustees of the Imperial War Museum, London; p16, John Spires, courtesy of Artists Incorporated; p17, private collection (left); courtesy of Paper Tiger, © Michael English (right); Butterfly Ball & The Grasshopper's Feast, © Alan Aldridge (bottom); p18, © Roger Dean (top), Spencer Paris courtesy of Artists Incorporated (bottom left), Gavin Macleod courtesy of Meiklejohn Illustration (right); p19, © Peter Stallard; pp20-21, The De Vilbiss Company Ltd; pp22-26, line drawings reproduced from *On the Spot Guides: Airbrush Maintenance* by Outline Press, © Peter Owen; pp24-25, The De Vilbiss Company Ltd; p70, courtesy of Dave and Gerry Bull; p71, courtesy of Paul Karslake.

Photography

p70 Tom Scott, p84 (bottom left and right), p92 (top left) and p94 by Henry Dobkin
pp28-31, 38-53, p55 (right), pp56-61, 95-96, 100-101 and p109 by Paul Forester

Special thanks to Keith Lockwood of Langford & Hill, London W1 for supplying all the graphic equipment; to Ian Bunker of The De Vilbiss Company Ltd; and to Jonathan Baker without whom this book would not have been possible. Additional thanks to Astrid Vargas Conte for her special warmth and generosity.

Contents

Chapter 1

Introduction

Although the airbrush has been around since the turn of the century, the very mention of the word can still create feelings of panic and fear. An incredible amount of mystique surrounds this tool. Not because it is such a highly sophisticated and complex feat of engineering — the principle and design have hardly changed at all throughout the years — but purely through a lack of knowledge.

Some colleges are introducing the airbrush into their curriculum, but the majority of practising professionals will tell you that they are 'self-taught'. The aim here is to cut through the 'aura' that has built up around this tool and demonstrate its usefulness. Over the following pages we trace the history of airbrushing, and how its popularity in specific areas evolved as people experimented.

The fact that you do not necessarily have to be a great artist to use an airbrush is illustrated by showing how you can create a beautiful image with the help of good reference material and a few tricks. Airbrushing is a technique and a process of building confidence. We hope to try to dispel some of the myths that have been built around the airbrush, and prove that it is one of the most versatile art forms of our time.

Introduction

HISTORY OF AIRBRUSHING

Through the symbols, engravings and painting of prehistoric man, we are not only made aware of our natural instinct to communicate visually, but of the earliest — albeit primitive — form of airbrushing. On the walls of the caves of Lascaux in southwest France there is a recurring image of the 'negative hand' created by Aurignacian man. Experts are positive that these images were created by placing the hand against the wall and painting around it. The texture of the paint shows that the area was sprayed by a primitive mouth diffuser, probably made from hollow bones.

This technique is still in use today, but the airbrush as we know it was first patented by Charles Burdick in 1893 in the UK. However, a patent for an airbrush case was registered in the USA in 1888. This must mean that a tool already existed to fit into it, and it is interesting to note that Burdick was an American who moved to the UK around that time. The reason for its development was most likely due to the invention of the daguerreotype. The problem with these 'instant pictures' was the poor quality of reproduction and the fact that they were monochrome. To overcome this, photographers were forced to retouch their end results. Although this was an improvement, it was by no means perfect and was painstakingly slow. The 'real artists', who were initially terrified of this new invention, began to relax when

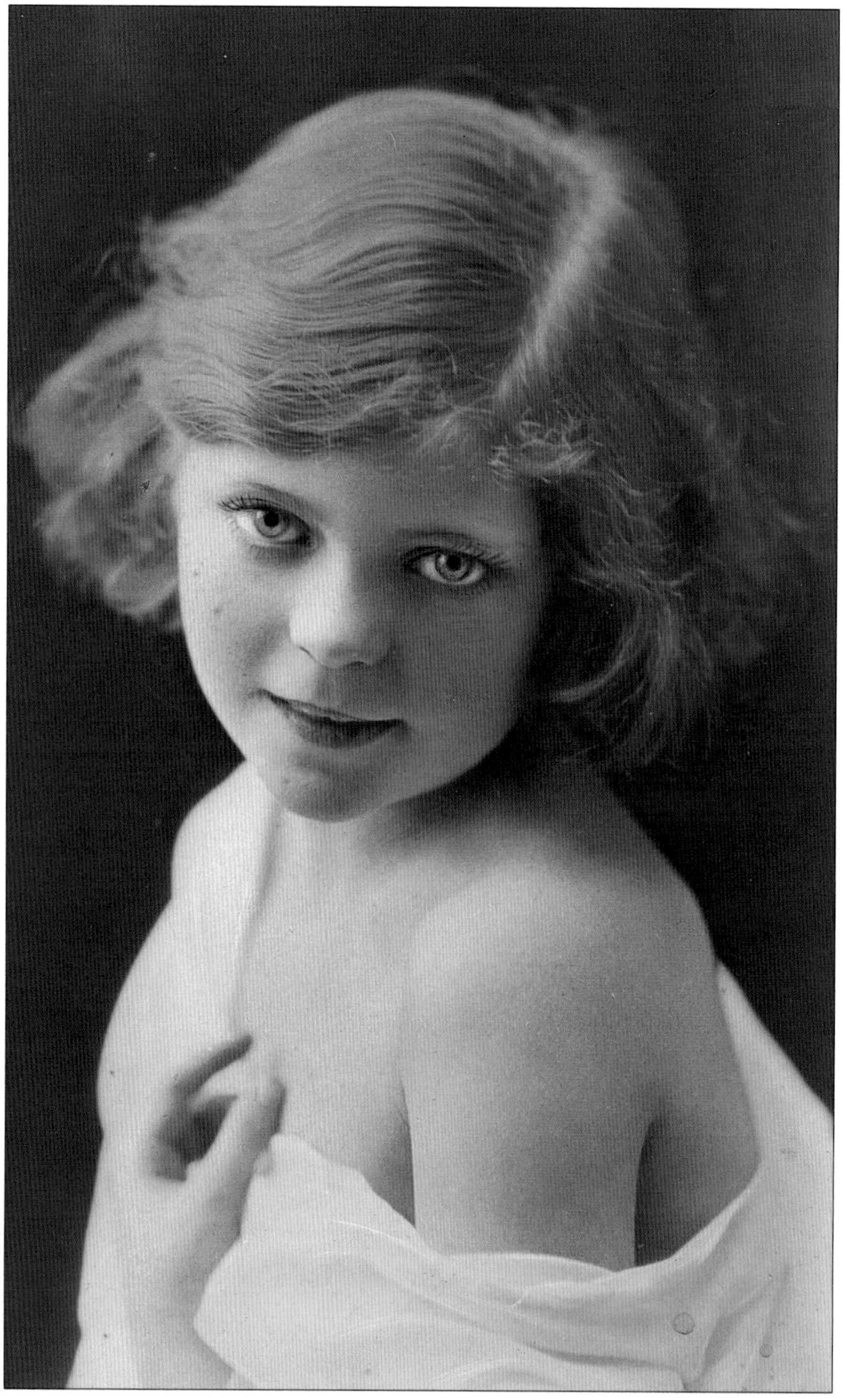

One of the earliest examples of colour tinting. Although details, such as the eyes and lips, are painted with a brush, the main body of this photograph was coloured with an airbrush. It is interesting to note that on the back of the picture, the photographer had recorded the colour of the girl's hair and eyes, even her type of complexion.

they saw these crude results that took so much trouble to achieve. However, due to the determination of the pioneers of photography, the airbrush was developed. Once this new tool was partnered with photography the end results were superb and even the 'old school of artists' was made to sit up and take notice.

Until the 1920s the airbrush was mainly used in photo-retouching, and it opened up huge possibilities for magazines and journals to illustrate stories successfully. In New York a magazine called *The World* sensationalised its crime reports by hiring actors to pose and re-create the 'fateful moment'. A photographer would then shoot the scene, and once developed the retoucher would erase the actors' faces, replacing them with those of the victims and accused. In London, with the invention of the halftone printing process, retouched photographs were good enough for reproduction, and *The London Illustrated Weekly* was the first to use them. From photographs to original artworks, it was clear that the smooth tones achieved by the airbrush were perfect for reproduction.

People were getting used to the fact that machines and technology were becoming part of everyday life, but no one forecast even in their wildest dreams the effect of an invention called the automobile. This was the making of the airbrush, for once the automobile was in mass production manufacturers needed to persuade the public to buy their particular model. The age of advertising was born.

To sell all these new machines to the masses a visual medium was required, and prior to the invention of television the poster was the most important form of advertising. The airbrush was ideal for depicting automobiles. The smooth shiny paintwork and chrome could be set against any particular background that the manufacturer chose.

Airbrushing could also make the cans look bigger, better and totally unused. The airbrush came into its own worldwide — no longer was it just the photo-retoucher's tool.

In Germany a group of artists banded together and formed a movement called the Bauhaus, with Walter Gropius, an architect, as director of the school. This was to be the single most important and influential group on visual communication through art and design, from when it first opened in 1919 to the present day. The group refused to accept the 'old-fashioned' view that there was a division between fine and applied arts — their aim was not just to sell products, but to create a style that would also bring art to the people. Surrounded by posters and billboards, 'Joe Public' was becoming much more visually conscious and aware. The school wanted to marry technology with

By Appointment to H.R.H. the Prince of Wales.
M.25.33
The deep power of the big engine . . . wildly exhilarating or beautifully docile at your lightest touch . . . the uplifting surge of this great car as you swing her over a hill . . . the quiet, happy drone when you put your foot down and the needle glides up and up . . . these are things to be felt, not just talked about . . . Have a word to-day with your local Morris dealer about trying the Morris '25' . . . without obligation, of course.
Three models from £385 : 0 : 0 ex works.
MORRIS '25'
Triplex glass & Dunlop Tyres standard.
MORRIS MOTORS, LTD., COWLEY, OXFORD.

Airbrushing allowed advertisers to show vehicles to their best advantage. By placing them against a plain background and using an unusual angle, attention was directed totally to the car, heightening its sophistication and smooth outlines.

art, bringing graphic design to the fore. Its members treated typography as an 'art' mixing it with photomontage and retouching, so that the airbrush — although dismissed by the 'old artists' — was thought highly of by the group. They treated the airbrush with great respect, experimented with it, and soon realised the incredible versatility of the tool. Students would visit the school and take their teachings back to their own countries. Bauhaus quickly reached the world.

One of the most important teachers at the Bauhaus school was Herbert Bayer. Previously a student of the school, his philosophy was that a good poster must be simple and direct, strong enough to command attention as well as conveying a message that must stick in the viewer's mind. The Nazis closed the school in 1933, but Bayer's influence carried on through his post as art director of the German *Vogue*. However with the imminent onset of war he, along with several others, migrated to the USA where his concepts and ideals were accepted with open arms.

E. McKnight Kauffer was an American artist who travelled and worked throughout Europe. Along with Cassandre in France, he is considered one of the first people to introduce symbolism into advertising, rather than merely presenting the products in a realistic way. In 1921 he returned to the USA with his 'new art', but at that time his efforts to convert the advertisers

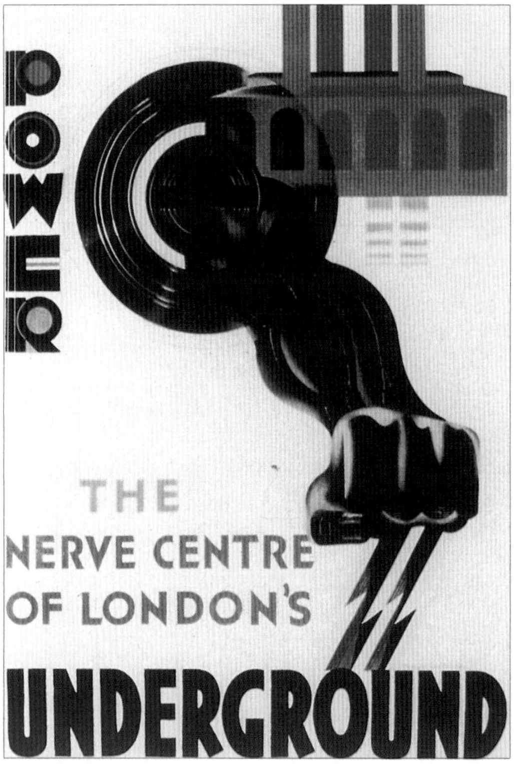

An example of E McKnight Kauffer's work for London Underground in 1930. By this period of his career, the images he produced had become very hard, almost surreal, and there was a very strong emphasis on typography.

Man Ray started to work with an airbrush as early as 1917. His experimentation was purely within the realms of black and white, and mainly surreal. This example of his work was commissioned by London

Right
Cassandre was one of France's most prolific poster artists. His use of the airbrush, and unique style, was striking enough to catch the eye of any passer-by, and to be copied the world over.

failed and so once again he returned to Europe. In London the director of London Underground's newly formed advertising department, Frank Pick, had noticed Kauffer's work and commissioned him for a whole series of travel posters that are now considered classics.

In Paris a Russian designer called Alexey Brodovitch, who had escaped his country's revolution, also came into his own with the new school of thought. He started as a set designer for the Ballet Russe, but was greeted with international acclaim when he won a major poster competition. In 1934 he was appointed art director of *Harper's Bazaar* where he stayed for 25 years, attracting such unknowns as Cocteau, Bresson and Penn to work for the magazine.

At this time in Vienna an artist by the name of Joseph Binder turned his hand to posters. Although airbrushing was incorporated into the 'new moderns' posters, Binder's work was depicted totally in airbrush. He went on to design corporate identities, creating company logos, trademarks and shop fronts. In 1922 he opened his own studio which, like the Bauhaus, was a place of pilgrimage for students worldwide. Ironically, through his airbrush work he developed tennis elbow and was forced to take some time off, and this made him turn his hand to teaching. In 1933 he was invited to lecture in the USA, but unlike Kauffer's unsuccessful return in 1921, America had now seen the birth of advertising and was ready for change.

By the 1930s manufacturers were making so many products that they could no longer handle all the advertising by themselves, prompting the first advertising agencies to set up. With the growth of advertising and the public demand for more sophisticated magazines, airbrush art went from strength to strength. At this time glamorous women were attracting notice everywhere, and with the rise of the motion picture — even though there was an economic depression — women, and life generally, were illustrated as 'perfect'.

The two main artists who specialised in depicting beautiful women were George Petty and Alberto Vargas. Petty's women were to be reproduced internationally, but were slightly stylised. Vargas, on the other hand, stuck to realism and perhaps this is why the airbrushed female form is always associated with Vargas. His was the 'all American girl', hence the expression 'the Varga Girl'. Vargas' illustrations appeared in many men's magazines, but were first popularised in *Esquire*. His were the ultimate pin-ups and when the Americans went to war, it was the Varga Girl who embellished the boy's planes and became a status symbol.

During the Second World War the poster artists turned to propaganda, and again the power of the poster was utilised, not to sell products, but to convey serious messages to the public. In England the most prolific of these 'war artists' was Abram Games. His images hit home and through his powerful style he could rouse, comfort, or tell people how they could help, these posters were as essential to the British people as Churchill himself.

Vargas will always be the king of the airbrushed pin-up — in his own words: 'What is more beautiful than a beautiful woman?' Although his popularity exploded in the 1930s and 40s, Vargas' expertise with the airbrush stemmed from his childhood when he used to watch his father — a famous South American photographer — use the tool for retouching. An airbrush to Vargas held no mysteries. To him it was just a part of everyday life.

In 1940 Walt Disney made *Pinocchio*, the most expensive animated film of the time. Here another use of the airbrush was discovered. It was perfect, not just for backgrounds, but for creating illusions of light by gradation. Even today the airbrush still plays a major role in animation.

The late 1940s and 50s were a quiet period for the airbrush. The world was recovering from a war, and with the advent of television as a new advertising medium, 'poster art' faded into the background. It was still widely used in animation, however, and, of course, for technical illustration, where airbrushing will always be important. Technical illustration really grew at the same time as advertising. People were not only interested in what the new machines they were buying looked like, but also how they worked. The man in the street did not necessarily grasp the highly technical workings of these machines, but an illustration added impact and held the customer in awe. Apart from the advertising side, technical illustration was useful for manufacturers. During this period, and still today, while a new engine or highly complex system is in the development stage, an artist will be employed to render the new mechanism from engineer's drawings to show potential trade customers or investors the ingenuity of the concept even pre-prototype, let alone production stage. Although this could not really be classed as creative, it still kept the airbrush busy, but its heyday seemed to have passed — or so most people in the know thought!

Suddenly in the 1960s a new revolution took place. Photography, which had taken over from the airbrush during the previous decade was considered too real and formal. From the mid-1960s, influenced by the use of hallucinatory drugs, the images for the new art posters were not just surreal, but went way beyond the stretches of the imagination. The airbrush was as popular then as it ever had been, and it was used not just for posters but for another new concept, the record sleeve.

The euphoric mood of the period was reflected in its music, and the world of pop music literally exploded. Groups were producing sounds which had never been heard before. Some were successful, others not, but the decade was all about

Above
This classic example of a war poster is in the Imperial War Museum, London. The strong image is the work of a French propagandist by the name of Sevek.

Right
Abram Games had a head start with airbrushing, following the example of his father who had used an airbrush for retouching. Games enlisted in the army in the Second World War, and when an artist was needed to work on war posters, the search was started by going through the list of recruits alphabetically. The first name to appear with any artist's experience was Games, and so his career was born.

experimentation so it did not matter. However the record was no longer just something to listen to, its packaging became important, with the mood of the music being reflected on the album cover. The idea was to look at the album sleeve while listening, hoping to find hidden messages or clues to the real meaning of the music. The Beatles were influential because as their career progressed so did their music, and they were established enough to be given a reasonably free rein. A full length, animated, psychedelic feature film was even created with the use of an airbrush around one of their songs, *Yellow Submarine*.

The mood continued throughout the early 1970s, although, as with all periods of wildness, life generally was beginning to settle down. Visual images also became calmer, and even though fantasy was still at the fore, the scenario was more of a fairy-tale nature. Many people who rejected conventional religion were searching for an alternative answer to life. Fantasy evolved into science fiction and with man's quest to reach other planets, so the representation in art was of UFOs and space beings. The airbrush proved its worth by being eminently capable of producing fantastic space scenes and landscapes, as well as depicting other life forms.

The popularity of the airbrush continued throughout the new, rather cold era of the materialistic 1980s. Money and possessions seemed to be the main aims of this decade, and because the masses no longer considered it obscene to accumulate wealth, advertising hit new peaks. Not only was the airbrush perfect for rendering gleaming technology, but manufacturers wanted hyper-realism again. This was not only restricted to objects, but because the airbrush was ideal for creating the subtle tones of skin, glamorous, long-legged women were illustrated to strengthen the idea that money could buy the perfect world.

As we move through the 1990s into a more caring world, the visual representations are softer once more, but the success of the airbrush keeps going from strength to strength. Its versatility has been more than proved, and the pioneers' dream of this very special tool being accepted across the board from graphic design to fine art has most definitely been realised. As for its future into the 21st Century, there is no looking back — the airbrush is here to stay.

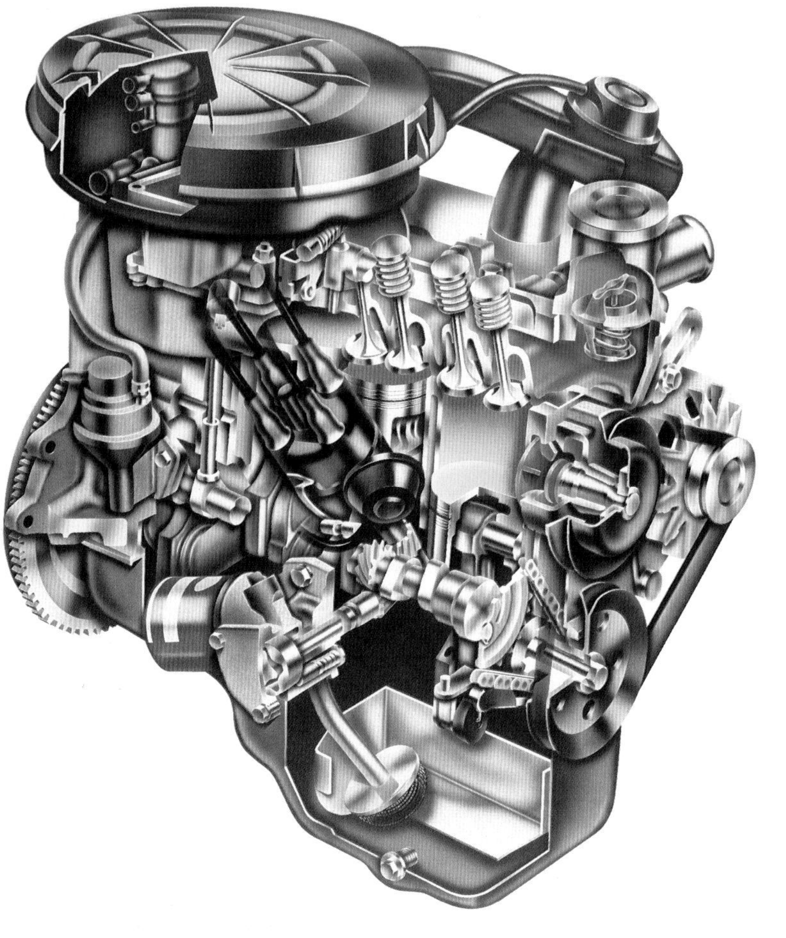

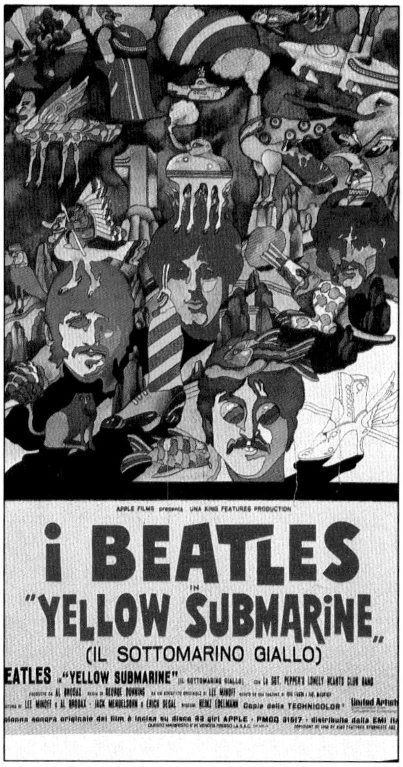

Michael English was one of the first UK artists of the 1960s to start experimenting with the airbrush. His initial inspiration came from the effects that could be achieved through silk screen printing. Due to his respected name he was partly responsible for the return to popularity of airbrushing. Posters were not just used to advertise products. Every pop concert, love-in or happening was publicised with a poster, and these became sought-after pieces of art. Michael English is now considered by the majority to be the best in the field.

The Beatles will always be remembered as the leaders of trends throughout the 1960s. Whatever whim or mood they moved into others followed. In the creation of the movie *Yellow Submarine*, inspired by their music, airbrushing was firmly established as a respected tool.

Left
John Spires' rendering of this British Ford Escort engine not only shows the high technology of this superb little engine, but somehow makes it more understandable. Note how he has accentuated the central power of this machine by colouring one of the cylinders with a 'red hot' glow.

Alan Aldridge in collaboration with Harry Willock produced a remarkable children's book in the early 1970s called *The Butterfly Ball*. Although loosely based on fairy stories, the images appealed to people of every age, and became quite a cult.

Roger Dean did not really make a name for himself as an illustrator until the beginning of the 1970s. It was while working on the seating — which he had designed — for Ronnie Scott's 'Upstairs' room that he was commissioned by a group called Gun for their first album cover. His early airbrush images were still highly influenced by the drug culture of the 1960s. Flying elephants!

Anything is possible in the field of science fiction, allowing the artist to put his or her imagination into overkill. Spencer Paris loves to specialise in this area. Even when he is designing a book jacket, he is simply given a copy of the manuscript and allowed to visually interpret the words himself.

The Porsche was considered the car of the 1980s. To own one was the ultimate status symbol, and made the statement, 'I am successful and have money.' This ethos was reflected perfectly by Gavin Macleod in this mean and moody image.

Right
The female figure, in whatever guise or form, will always be one of the most popular images with artists. In this example, Peter Stallard, a resident of Colorado, shows how versatile the airbrush can be. Not only does he depict perfect skin tones, but manages to introduce a whole range of effects and textures into the image. Stone, sky, foliage and water are all included, proving once and for all the versatility of the airbrush.

Chapter 2

The Airbrush

The basic principle of the airbrush has changed little since it was first introduced in the 1890s. It is a mechanical tool which mixes air with paint and propels the fine spray produced by this combination onto the chosen support. All airbrushes are pen-shaped, have a fine internal needle, a nozzle where the air and paint are mixed and a receptacle for the colour. A rubber hose connects the airbrush to the chosen air supply which is in turn controlled by a lever or push button.

However, these days there are many variations on the theme — not just in the choice of airbrushes themselves, but in the source of the air supply. Rather than get side-tracked with every conceivable model and any individual manufacturer's modifications, which would be so easy, let us concentrate here on the three main types of airbrush which will suffice for most people's needs — these being the single-action, fixed double-action and independent double-action airbrushes.

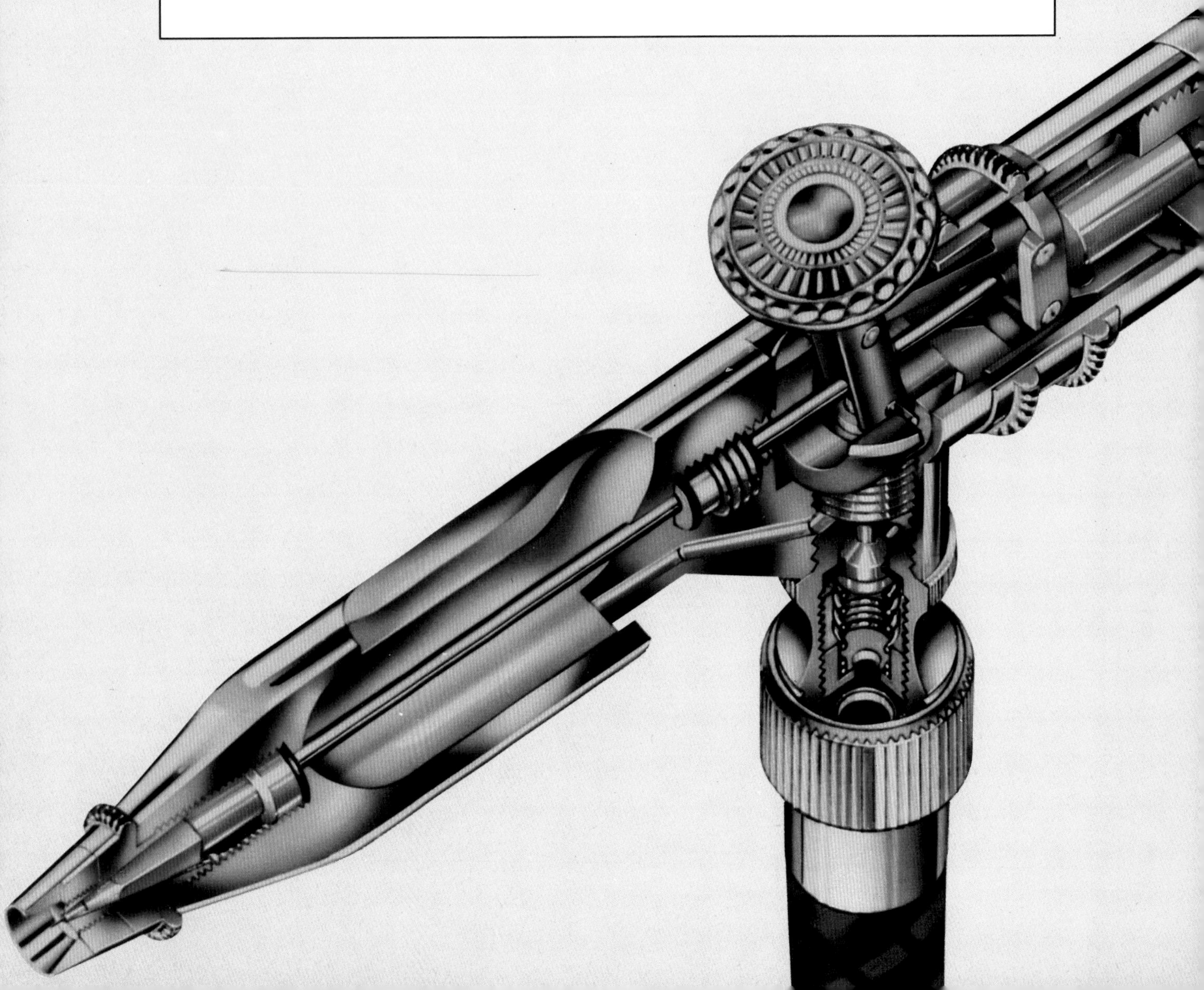

PER 63

The Airbrush

SINGLE ACTION AIRBRUSH

This is the simplest and cheapest type of airbrush. It has a single on/off trigger for the air supply. Therefore, while using the airbrush, you have no control over the amount of air drawn into the airbrush or the ratio of air to paint. Most single-action airbrushes allow you to adjust the paint volume, but this is only possible when you are not spraying. To adjust the spray pattern and the density of spray while using a single-action you must alter the distance between the airbrush and the support. The most basic single-action airbrushes have an 'external mix' operation (top right). The air from the airbrush blows across the end of the tube which supplies the paint and this draws the paint into the air stream. Unfortunately the paint often does not atomize completely and the result is a rather rough spray.

To overcome this problem there are also 'internal mix' single-action airbrushes (bottom right) which mix the paint with the air as it flows through the body of the airbrush itself. These provide a much better spray quality but are far more expensive and do not really match a cheap double-action airbrush for value.

On the whole the single-action airbrush is fine for laying flat colours, but it is a very limited tool and does not allow the beginner to progress far.

Single-Action Airbrush

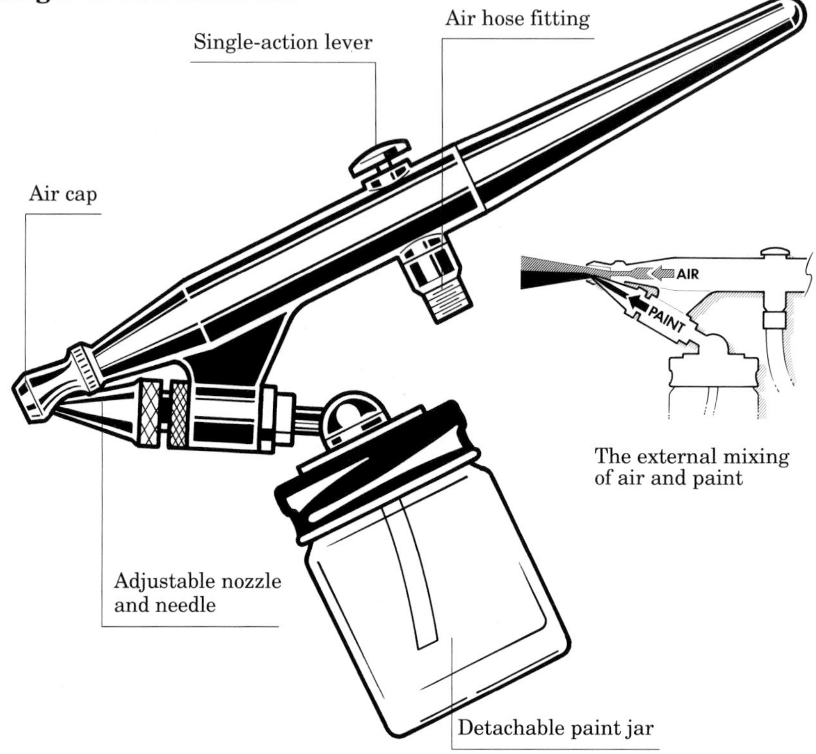

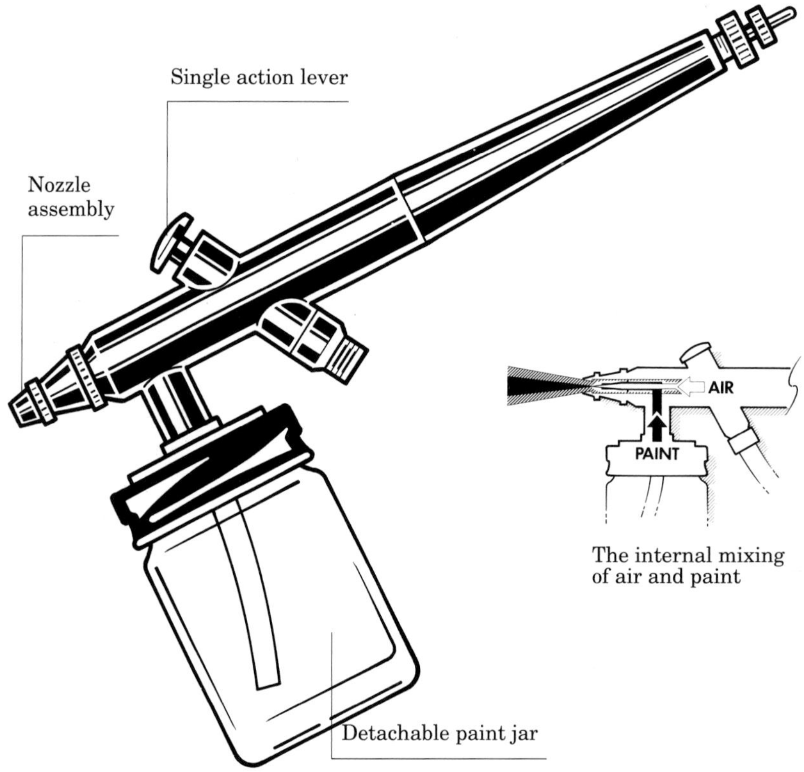

Fixed Double-Action Airbrush

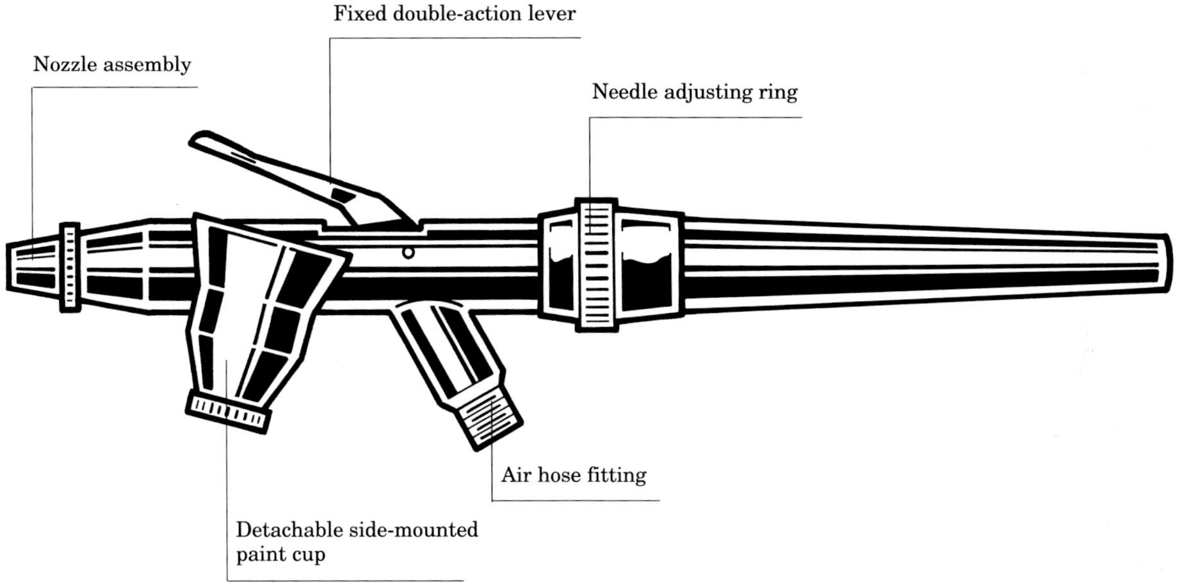

There are very few fixed double-action airbrushes on the market, but they do offer distinct advantages over the single-actions. A single trigger controls the flow of both paint and air. It is pushed down to release the air and then pulled back to draw the needle back in the nozzle and so release paint into the air stream. Although the spray is reliable and even, the relationship between air and paint is fixed while in use. Some models do allow you to pre-set the ratio of paint to air before you begin spraying, and occasionally a ring is provided which allows you to determine the width of spray from a hairline right up to a broad sprayed line.

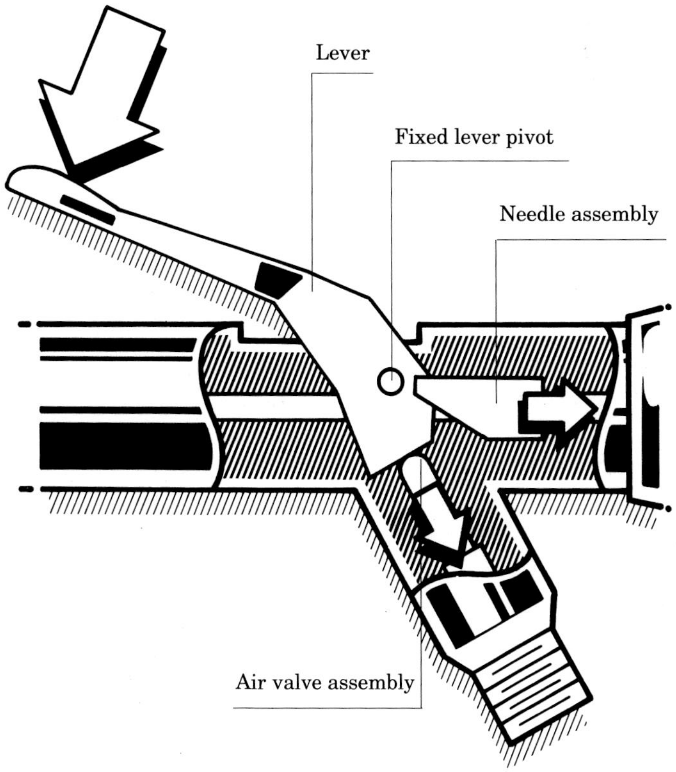

Independent Double-Action Airbrush

By far the most versatile and popular type of airbrush is the independent double-action. It has a similar trigger assembly as the fixed double-action, but gives you complete control over the amount of air flowing through the airbrush, and the amount of colour which it sprays. Once mastered you can switch from the finest of washes to a dense, solid colour in a single sweep.

Most models have an adjusting screw or cam ring which fixes the trigger at a certain point, so if you wish it can be used as a fixed double-action airbrush.

An independent double-action airbrush has been used for all the step-by-step instructions in this book, and although more expensive than other types, it is well worth investing the extra money into a tool which, if looked after correctly, will serve you well for years to come.

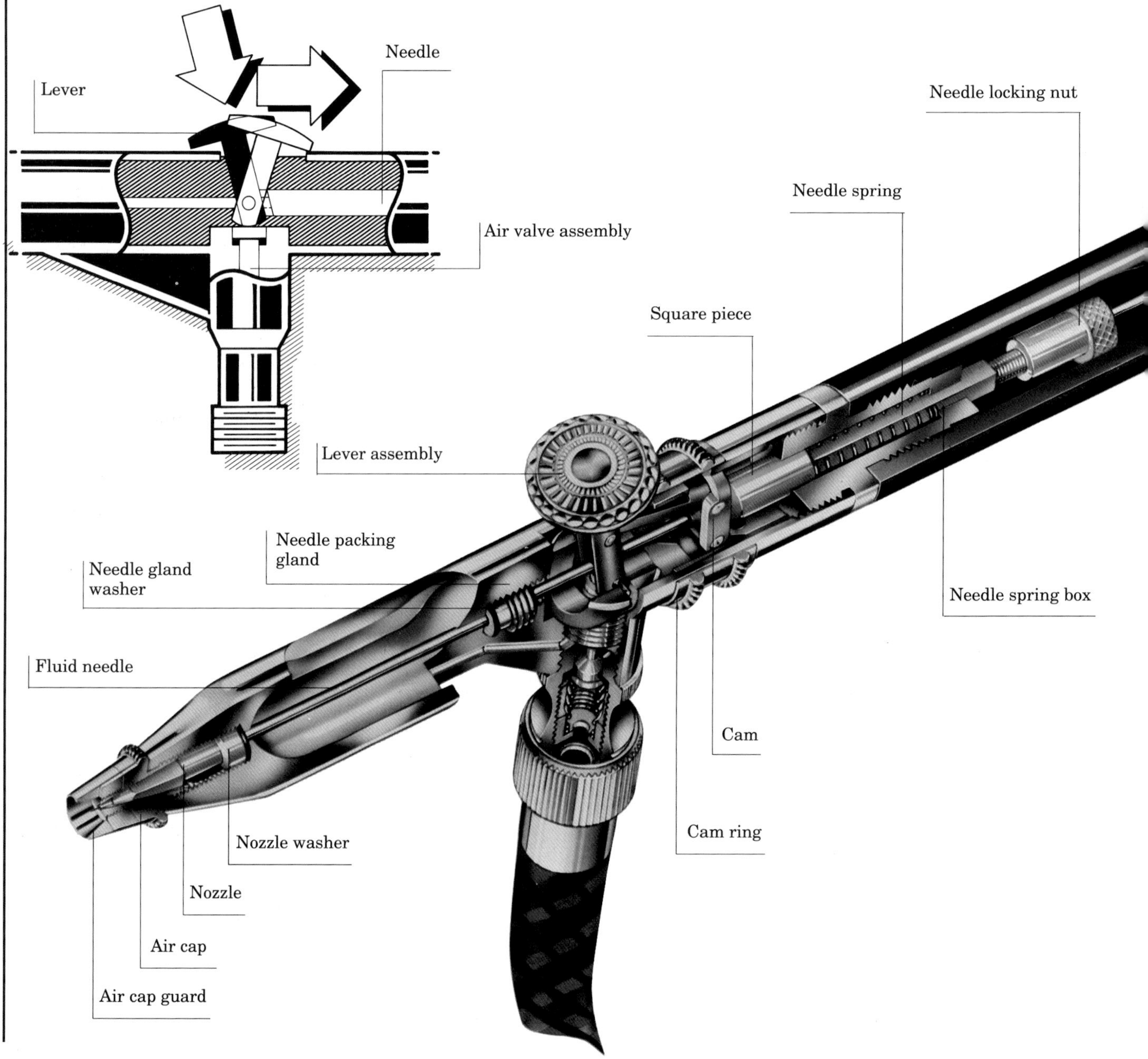

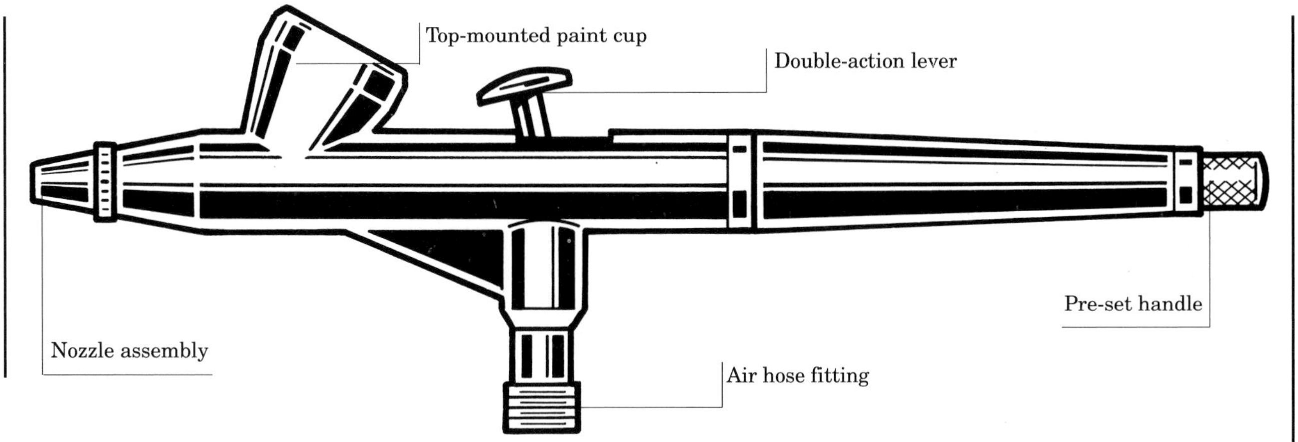

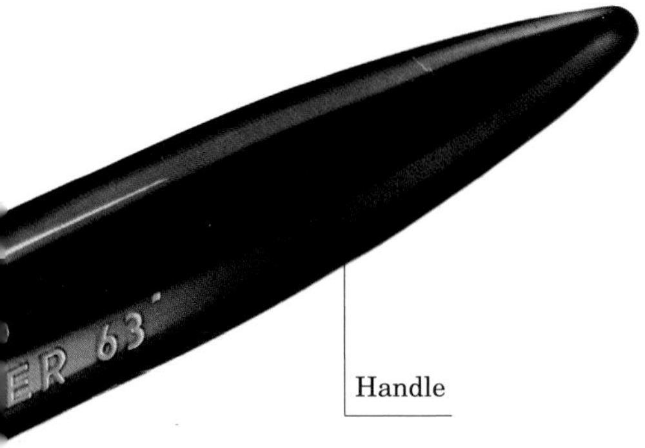

Reservoirs

Another consideration when selecting an airbrush is the placing of the paint reservoir. Paint is drawn into the airbrush in one of two ways — gravity feed or suction feed — and the reservoir placing and size of reservoir depends on which principle is used.

With suction feed the paint is drawn up from a reservoir below the body of the airbrush. The advantages of suction-feed airbrush are that the reservoir can have a large capacity, it can be easily removed and changed for one holding a different colour, and, since removable, it is easy to clean. They do have the disadvantage though of being cumbersome to use since the reservoir can easily get in the way for close up work.

With gravity-feed airbrushes the reservoir is either mounted on the top or to one side of the airbrush body. They have a more limited liquid capacity and the reservoir is often inseparable from the airbrush body, which means that they must be cleaned out thoroughly between each colour change. However, they are better balanced, and so ideal for detailed work where good airbrush control is required.

Suction feed

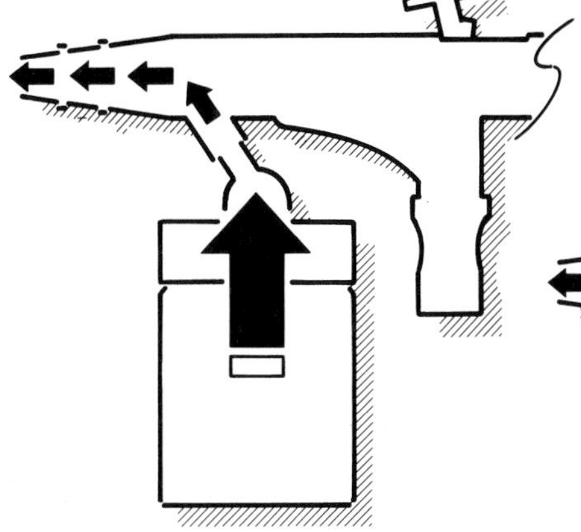

Gravity feed

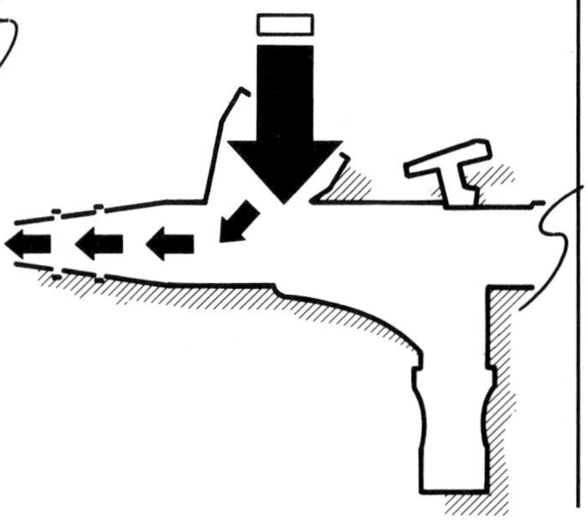

Air Sources

Almost as important as your choice of airbrush is that of your air supply. An inadequate air supply can be a severe detriment to even the most expensive airbrush. If money is tight, however, priority should be given to the airbrush since there are cheap air supplies which can be used until you can afford a good compressor.

At the very bottom of the range, and definitely not recommended, is the car tyre (where the air line is attached to the valve on a partially inflated tyre) or the foot pump and tank. Both give a very limited supply of air and are incredibly unreliable due to the lack of control.

Air Cans

For newcomers to airbrushing compressed air cans are a relatively cheap way to get the feel of your airbrush before moving up to better things, and can prove useful if you need to airbrush away from your base. However, in the long term these are just not economical, and they have the major drawback of gradually losing pressure as they empty. In fact an air can could easily run out at a crucial moment — very frustrating to say the least.

Air Cylinders

Large cylinders of compressed air, which have an air hose attachment and a pressure regulator, can be bought or hired. They are much longer lasting and more economical than cans since they can usually be refilled once they have run out, but they are very cumbersome and in the long run still work out more expensive than a compressor.

Compressors

If you intend to do a lot of airbrushing it is wise to invest in a good air compressor. Prices vary tremendously, but to achieve the ideal of a constant, regulated flow of moisture-free air three vital elements are necessary. First, the compressor must have a moisture trap to extract humidity from the generated air, otherwise drops of condensation can form, work their way up the air line and onto your artwork. Second, it needs a pressure regulator since thicker paints require a higher air pressure and low air pressures can be used to create some interesting spatter effects. Third, make sure it has a pressure gauge (often found as part of the regulator) so that operating levels can always be checked - the normal operating pressure is 15–40 psi (1–2.6 bar).

There are two main types of compressor — the direct and the tank.

Direct Compressors

These are the most basic, and therefore the cheapest, compressors. An electric motor fitted with a diaphragm pumps air directly into the air hose.

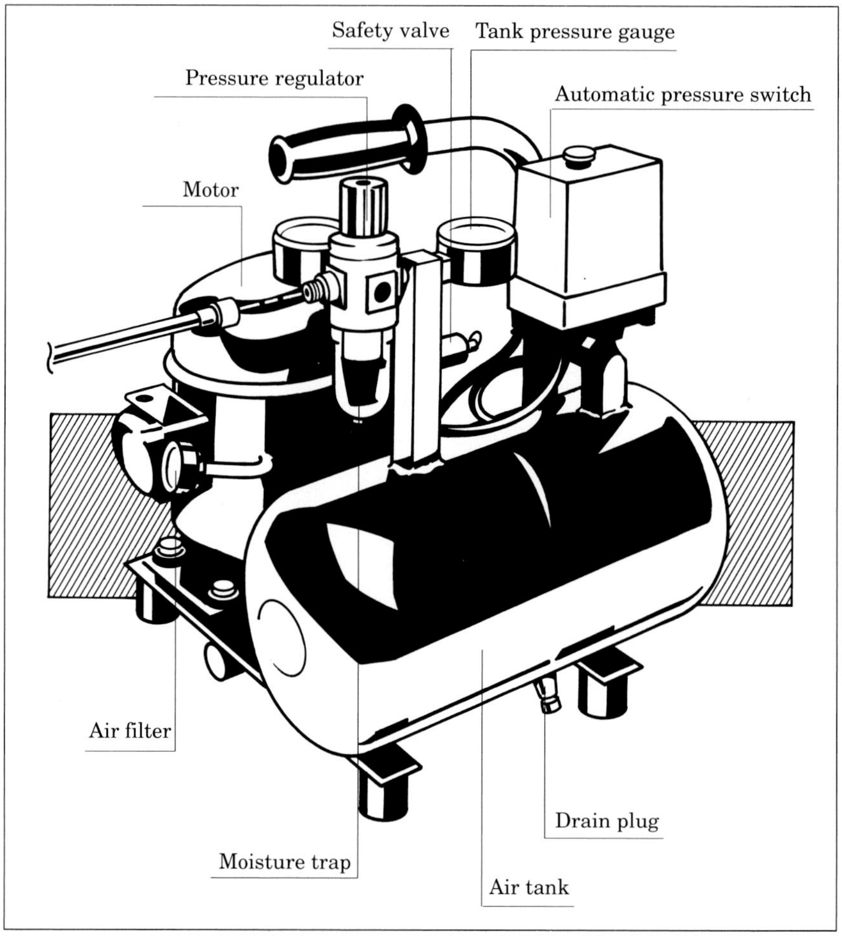

Unfortunately, as it does this the diaphragm creates a pulsing air flow which makes the quality of the spray vary. In addition moisture traps and pressure regulators are rarely incorporated, and so these cannot really be recommended for fine or detailed work.

Tank Compressors

Modern tank compressors are generally quiet, maintain a constant air pressure, and have a moisture trap, but are notably more expensive than direct compressors. This design pumps air into a storage tank from where it is drawn into the air hose as a constant, non-pulsing supply at a steady, but adjustable pressure. The motor switches on and off to keep the supply of air topped up and to keep the pressure in the tank at a level higher than that required, which means that the air supply is very reliable and constant. Tank compressors can be pricey, but really are essential for achieving a professional-looking piece of art.

Having probably spent a substantial amount of money on your airbrush it is important that you learn how to look after it correctly. A properly maintained airbrush could easily serve you for many years to come. Although an extremely delicate tool, the airbrush is in fact relatively easy to service and maintain — the golden rule here is to always keep it clean. Dust, moisture and hardened paint can all clog up your airbrush, so it is important to get into the routine — albeit a boring one — of cleaning your airbrush regularly. Do this only at the end of every session and when changing colours, but even if you have to leave it for a very short period of time, especially if you are using a fast-drying medium such as waterproof inks.

Flushing Through

Between every colour change and after every working session it is imperative to clean your airbrush by flushing through. Pour any paint left in the reservoir into a container for future use. Wipe away any spots of paint still in the reservoir with a small paint brush, and then spray off any remaining paint onto a scrap of paper or into a tissue. Continue spraying until the air stream is totally clear. There will probably still be tiny amounts of paint lurking inside your airbrush so fill the reservoir with water (or the appropriate solvent for non-

Wiping away any paint left in the reservoir with an old paint brush.

water based paints) and again spray through onto a scrap of paper. Carry on filling the reservoir and spraying through until you are absolutely sure there is nothing left inside your airbrush. However tired you are make sure you do a thorough job or the next time you use your airbrush you could be in for a nasty shock.

Filling the reservoir with water.

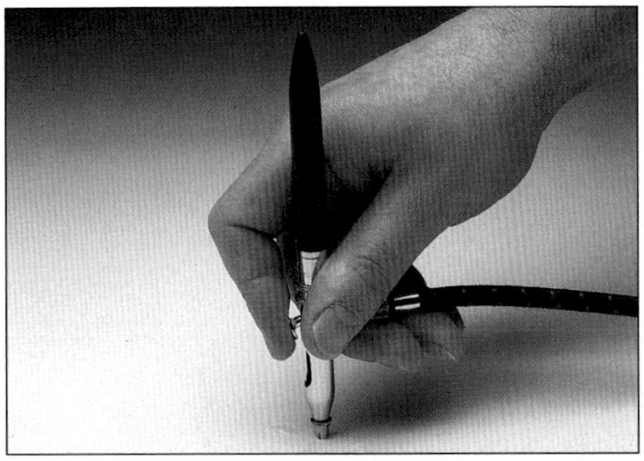

Spraying the water through onto an old piece of paper. If space is limited, instead of spraying through onto a piece of paper and risking stray droplets landing on your artwork, a plastic bag held around the end of your airbrush will do just as well.

CLEANING THE NEEDLE

The needle is one of the most delicate parts of your airbrush and must be treated with great regard. Although it is replaceable, with a little care and attention it can actually be made to last for quite some time.

1 Unscrew the casing of your airbrush and loosen the exposed needle locking nut.

2 Now very carefully withdraw the needle from the airbrush.

1

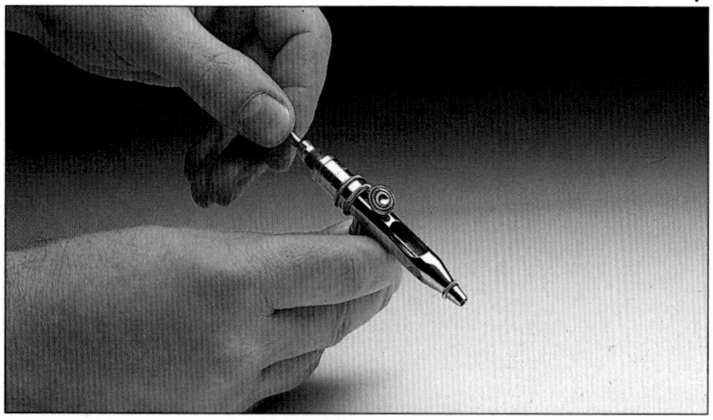

2

3

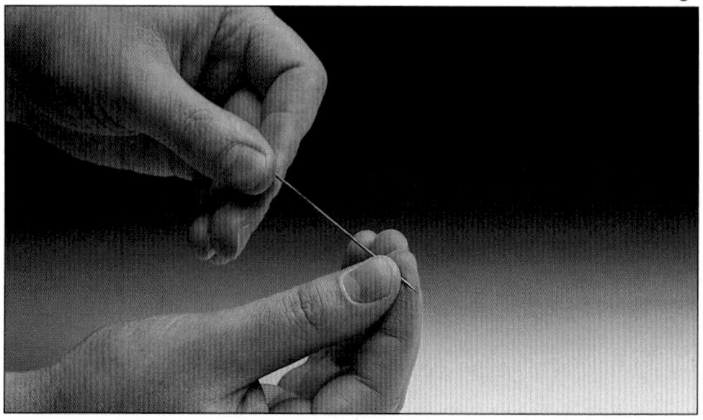

4

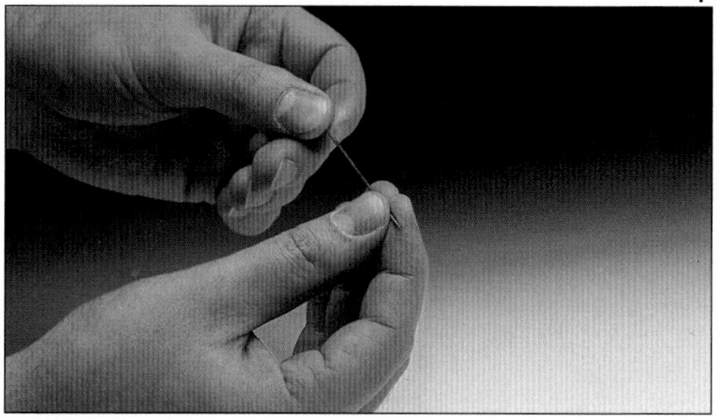

5

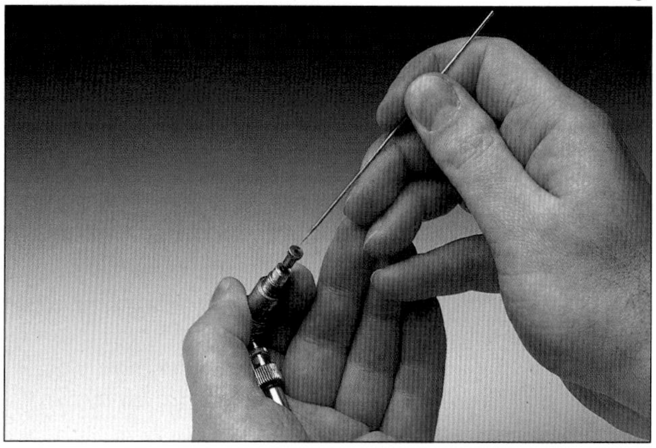

3 Dampen your fingers with a tiny amount of water, hold the needle carefully as shown here, and then very gently roll it between your fingers to remove any dirt. Alternatively, the needle can be rolled very lightly on a piece of detail paper since this has a slightly abrasive surface. Under no circumstances put any pressure on the needle because this could easily bend it out of shape and impair its performance.

4 Do a thorough examination of your needle to make sure that it is not damaged. If there are any bends, or the tip is blunt, replace the needle with a new one at once.

5 Make sure the lever control button of your airbrush is forward and down, and then very carefully re-insert the needle into the airbrush, resting the shaft on one fingertip, and pushing it in slowly until it stops naturally. You can then replace the locking nut and casing, screwing both only finger tight.

After the needle, the nozzle is the most fragile part of your airbrush. Its life expectancy can be greatly increased so long as you get into the habit of cleaning it regularly. Although the following routine applies for most independent double-action airbrushes — those with 'floating' nozzles — always check with the instructions that came with your airbrush for any differences in method.

1 Unscrew the airbrush casing and loosen the needle locking nut. You do not need to remove the needle completely, but to avoid bending it, carefully pull it back and re-tighten the locking nut to hold it in place.

2 Unscrew and remove the air cap, and then separate it from the air cap guard. The floating nozzle, complete with its small, black washer, can now be removed. Put this to one side to be dealt with in a moment.

3 Dampen your thumb with a little water, and then gently rub the air cap clean. It is also a good idea to check the air cap carefully at this point to make sure that it is undamaged.

4 Using an old brush you now meticulously clean the air cap guard, making sure that there are no traces of paint hiding inside it.

5 Pull the tiny washer off the nozzle and put it aside in a safe place. The nozzle itself is cleansed by soaking it in water (or an appropriate solvent if using non-water based paints). If there are any traces of paint still lurking inside it, get an old straight airbrush needle and very softly turn it inside the nozzle until none remains. Check the nozzle for signs of damage, and if there are any replace it. Otherwise refit the black washer and firmly seat the nozzle back in the airbrush. The air cap and air cap guard are now replaced onto the airbrush. Loosen the needle locking nut, gently push the needle forward until it stops, and re-tighten the locking nut. You can then finally screw the casing back on.

1

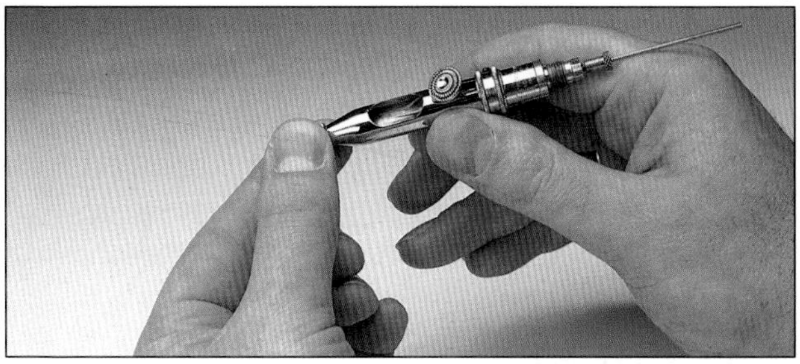

2

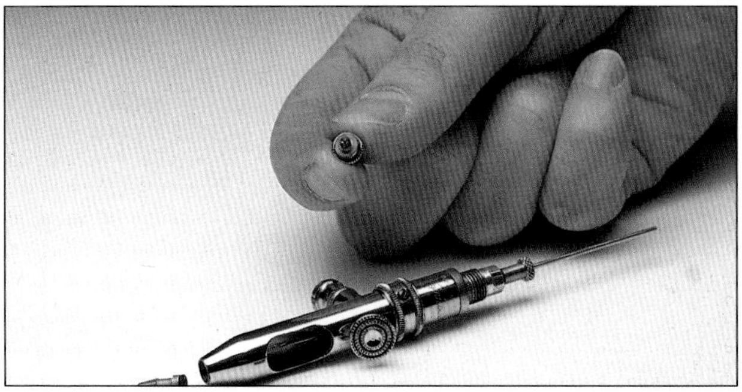

3

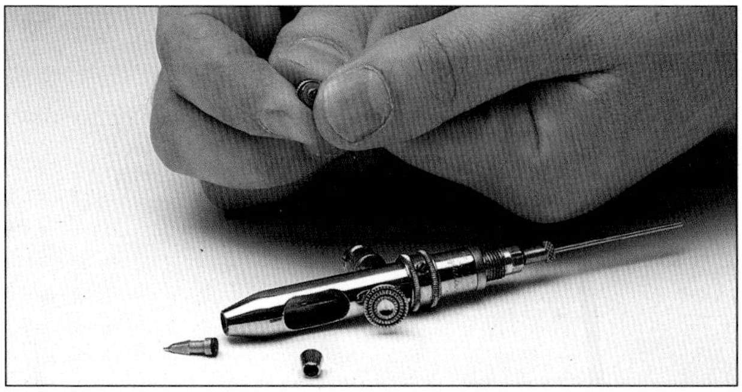

4

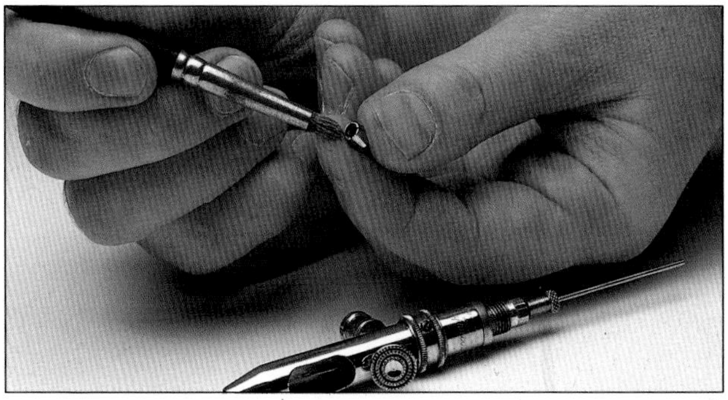

5

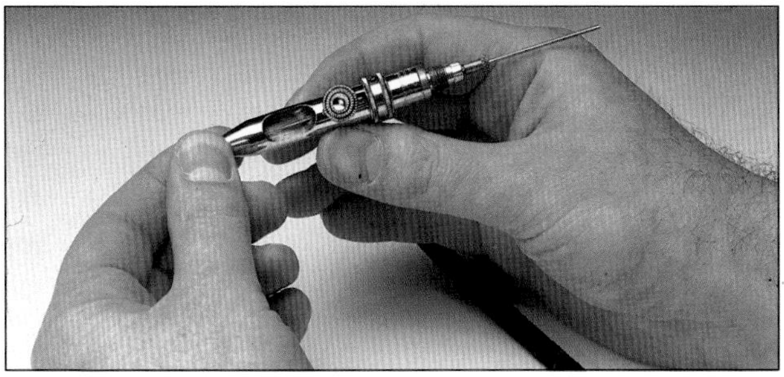

Fault Finding Chart

THE AIRBRUSH

Problem		Analysis	Cure
No air flow	1	Something turned off at compressor	Check compressor
	2	Damaged or incorrectly positioned spray head washer or nozzle washer	Replace or refit
	3	Air-feed in airbrush blocked	Empty, remove nozzle and blast air through airbrush; check diaphragm assembly on air valve
	4	Lever assembly broken	Replace (professional repair)
	5	Air valve stem broken	Replace (professional repair)
	6	Blockage in air supply from compressor	Remove airbrush from lead and blow at high pressure
	7	Air valve seat faulty	Replace
Air leaks through nozzle	1	Air valve springs and valve seal incorrectly tensioned	Readjust or replace when airbrush turned off
	2	Diaphragm assembly and air valve stem or ball incorrectly adjusted	(professional repair)
Air leaks through control lever	1	Diaphragm assembly broken	Replace (professional repair)
Air leaks at source	1	Connections loose	Tighten
	2	Adaptor not screwed tight enough	Screw down
	3	Washer in hose or connections worn	Replace
Air blast out at very high pressure	1	Pressure at compressor set too high	Turn down control
Medium not spraying	1	No medium in reservoir	Fill reservoir
	2	Nozzle too far from air supply	Adjust nozzle
	3	Paint too thick/badly mixed	Empty and clean; remix paint
	4	Feed tube not immersed in medium	Add more medium
	5	Medium flow from container blocked	Clean
	6	Medium has dried on nozzle	Remove and clean nozzle and needle; check nut attaching control lever needle is tight
	7	Needle wedged in nozzle	Reset carefully and check needle and nozzle locking nut
	8	Pigment settled in medium	Run through with thinner, and agitate the needle
	9	Lever to needle locking nut loose	Tighten
	10	Lever assembly broken	Replace (professional repair)

Problem		Analysis	Cure
Medium not spraying and/or bubbles in reservoir and/or spatter	1	Nozzle cap loose	Tighten
	2	Badly seated nozzle	Remove and re-seat
	3	Nozzle washer missing	Replace
	4	Bad match of nozzle and nozzle cap	Replace one or both
	5	Damaged or split nozzle	Replace
Medium leaks from reservoir	1	Airbrush held at an angle allowing medium out of reservoir	Hold airbrush level
	2	Washers & joints badly seated or tightened	Re-set
	3	Nozzle washer missing or damaged	Replace
	4	Needle set too far back when not in use	Turn forward after use
Medium escapes from nozzle during use	1	Air supply inadequate	Increase air or decrease medium
	2	Nozzle cap loose	Tighten
	3	Medium escaping from reservoir and running onto the nozzle	Hold airbrush level
Medium flooding	1	Medium too thin	Remix
	2	Needle too far back	Reset needle further forward; use needle more gently; reset lever action
	3	Nozzle or paint tube set too high	Adjust
Dirty medium colour	1	Reservoir, feed, nozzle or nozzle cap dirty	Clean
Lever fails to return after pressing down	1	Air valve spring has lost its tension	Stretch if possible or replace
	2	Sticky air valve stem	Strip and clean
Lever flops or fails to return after pulling back	1	Needle spring stuck or has lost its tension	Re-tension spring; clean and re-lubricate
	2	Lever assembly broken	Replace (professional repair)
Needle fails to return after being pulled back	1	Needle locking nut loose	Tighten
	2	Needle packing gland gripping on needle	Slacken needle packing gland screw; clean needle and lubricate
	3	Needle will not go through packing gland	Loosen packing gland screw and clean
Knocking noise at rear when moving forward	1	The balance weight at the end of the airbrush has become loose and is knocking the needle	Remove handle and push weight into place

Problem		Analysis	Cure
Spatter or spitting *see illustration 1*	1	Inadequate air pressure for medium	Adjust air pressure
	2	Dust in nozzle	Remove and clean
	3	Badly mixed medium - too thick	Empty and clean; remix
	4	Build-up of medium in nozzle cap	Make sure needle is firm. Clean with brush thinners
	5	Worn, cracked or split nozzle	Replace
	6	Bad match of nozzle and needle	Replace one or both
	7	Dirt or excess moisture in air supply	Remove nozzle and blast air through; check filter at air source
	8	Medium clogging air feed	Replace worn air valve washer; repair diaphragm assembly (professional repair)
	9	Medium has seeped into handle aperture which has caused the diaphragm assembly to break	Replace diaphragm assembly (professional repair)
Spatter at an angle *see illustration 2*	1	Split nozzle or bent needle	Replace
Spatter at start of strokes *see illustration 3*	1	Build-up of medium caused by lever being returned too quickly	Release lever more gently
	2	Damaged needle	Replace
	3	Medium build-up in nozzle cap	Make sure needle is firm. Clean with brush thinners
	4	Dust in nozzle	Remove and clean
	5	Excess moisture or impurities in air line	Remove nozzle and blast through with air; check filter at air supply
Spatter at end of strokes *see illustration 4*	1	Excess moisture or impurities in air line	Remove nozzle and blast through with air; check filter at air supply
	2	Damaged needle or damaged or dirty nozzle	Replace or clean
Blobs at either end of stroke *see illustration 5*	1	Hand stationary at start or end of stroke	Move hand both before and after operating the trigger
	2	Lever not eased in time	Practise makes perfect
	3	Medium released before air	Reset lever action
Uneven strokes or flaring *see illustration 6*	1	Airbrush being operated from wrist	Use whole arm
	2	Dust in nozzle	Remove nozzle and clean

Problem		Analysis	Cure
Spidery effect *see illustration 7*	1	Airbrush too close to support for nozzle or needle setting	Move away or adjust
	2	Too much medium	Adjust control lever to correct air to medium ratio
	3	Medium released before air	Reset lever action
Pulsating spray pattern *see illustration 8*	1	Pulsating air supply due to a small compressor without a tank	Add a pressure regulator to your compressor
	2	Dust in nozzle	Remove nozzle and clean
	3	Badly seated nozzle or nozzle cap	Check and adjust
	4	Nozzle washer worn	Replace
Fine line appearing with slight haze *see illustration 9*	1	Damaged or bent needle	Replace

1

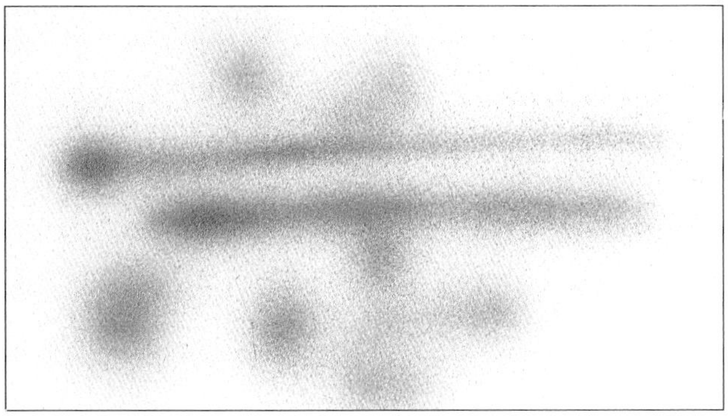

2

3

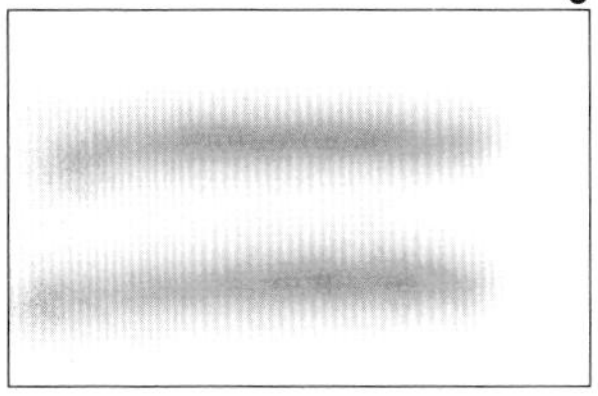

4

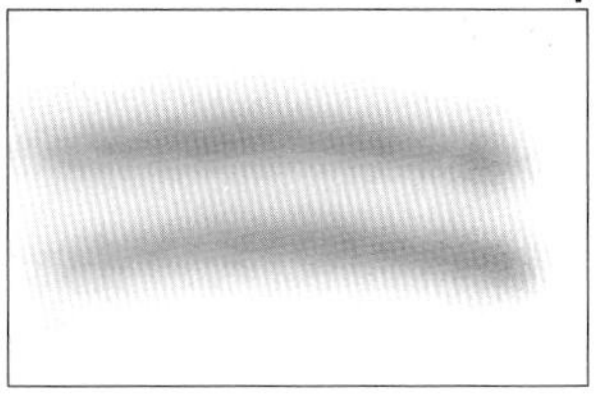

5

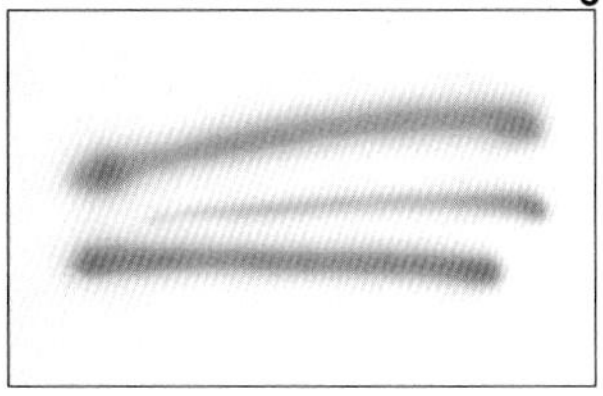

6

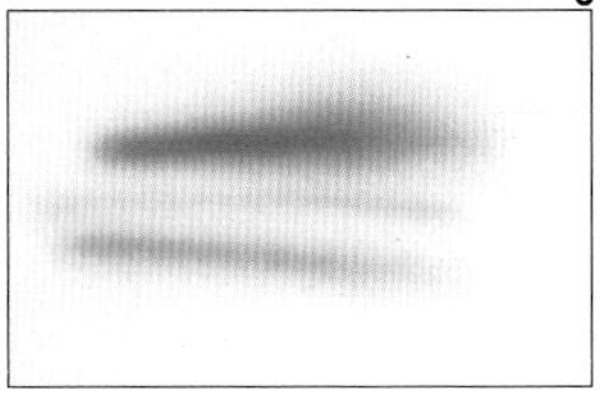

7

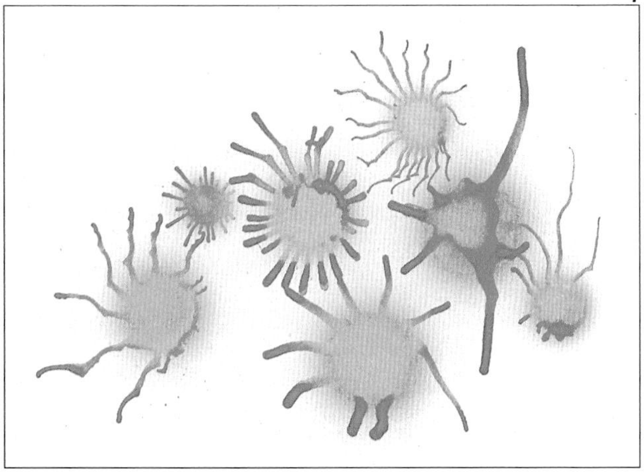

8

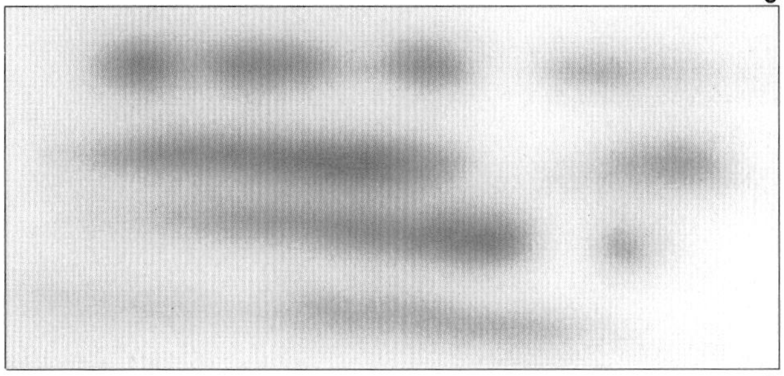

9

Chapter 3

Before you spray

Although you must be itching to actually start using your airbrush, there is some very useful equipment which should be included in your kit. For me a graphic supply shop is the equivalent of an Aladdin's cave. The rows of paints, coloured pencils and papers are not only enough to inspire anyone to take up painting, but unfortunately to also spend a great deal of money on equipment of which we might never make use.

When venturing into any new field it is always best to just start with the necessities, especially in airbrushing as you have probably spent a small fortune on your actual airbrush. If your background is in the world or art or design you should not really need to buy anything new. However, as with most things, it is not until you physically start that you begin to become aware of odd things that could prove extremely useful. So resist temptation, and gradually build up your kit as and when you need particular items and save the luxuries for the Christmas list. The items which are included here will all be put to good use and are relevant to your needs as an aspiring airbrush artist.

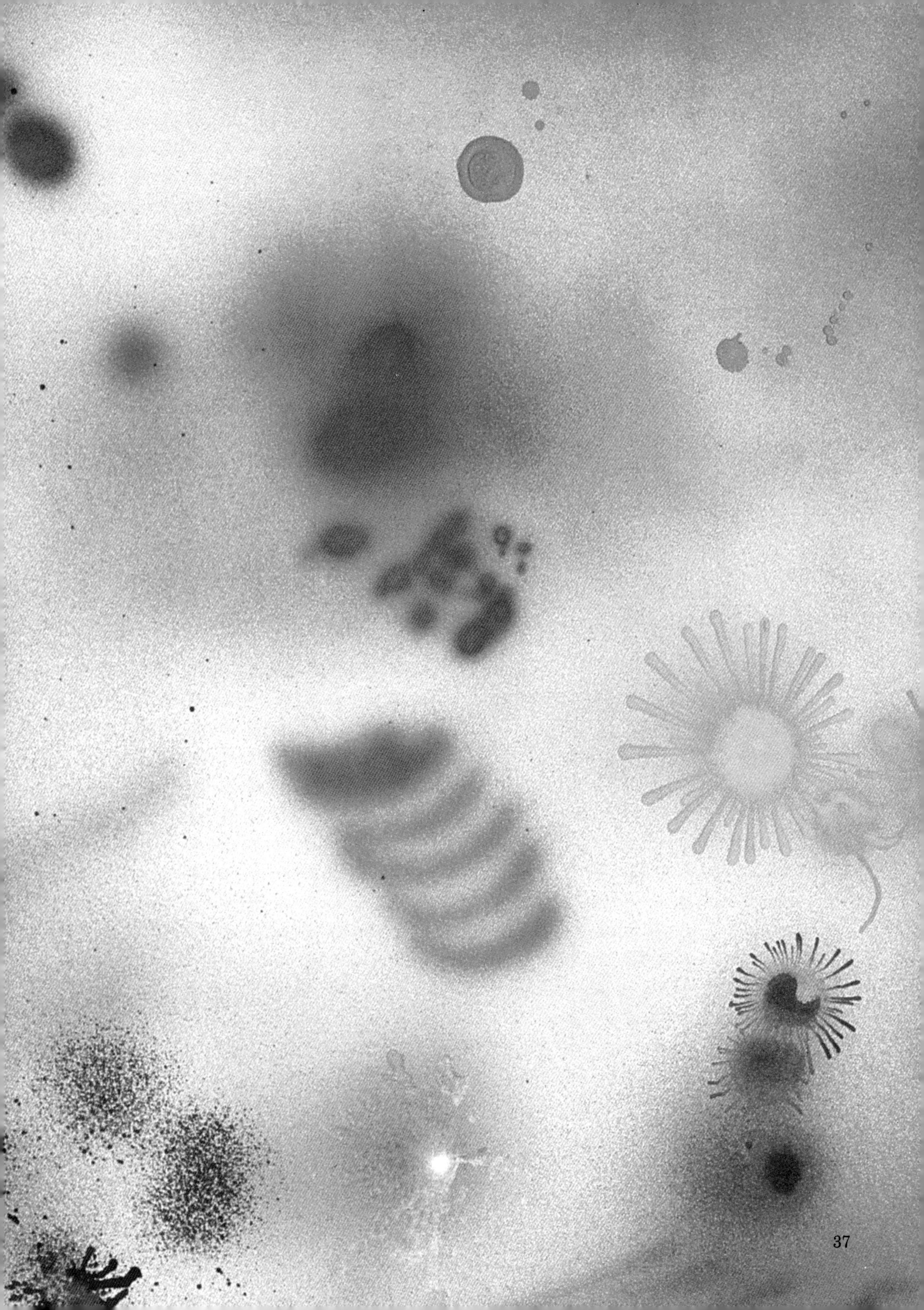

A good cutting mat is essential for cutting masks. The best types are printed with a grid which enables you to keep an instant check on accuracy. Some are translucent, so if you have access to a light box this is an added bonus.

Craft knives and scalpels are obviously necessary for mask cutting, but even more importantly always keep a good supply of new blades. The blades must be changed regularly to ensure a clean cut for your masks.

There are two different rulers worth purchasing — clear plastic is useful so that while you are using it the artwork is still visible, and a solid metal rule for use when cutting straight-edged masks since the blade will not damage the edge.

Compasses create perfect circles and a pair of dividers will transfer measurements from your reference to the support.

The most useful drawing aid is a set of clear plastic templates called French curves. These are designed to incorporate as many different degrees of curve as possible. Another invaluable aid is a flexible curve which is basically a flexible strip which will hold any shape that it has been bent into.

You will, of course, need selection of hard to soft leaded pencils for tracing and drawing the image. But where line work is incorporated in an artwork a technical pen will achieve lines of a constant width. Water-soluble crayons are also useful and felt-tip pens are a quick way to work out your colour scheme on a rough visual.

Erasers will not just erase unwanted pencil marks from your artwork — a stick eraser can be used to remove paint and so create highlights.

A set of sable brushes for adding fine detail will never go amiss, and cheap bristle brushes are very handy for mixing paint. A ceramic palette is rather a luxury for combining colours, and can be bought at a later stage — saucers and old cups are just as good.

Last, but not least, you will need a supply of masking tape, cleaning solvent for the airbrush, and lighter fuel for removing any marks from the support.

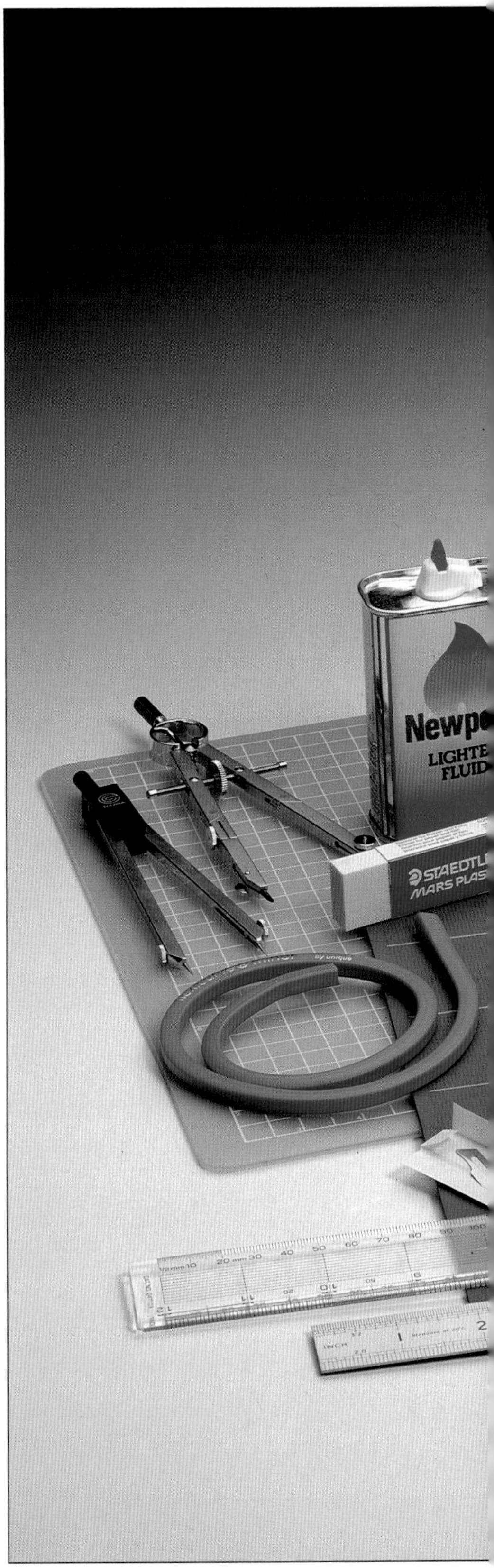

3M
Spray Mount
Allows for repositioning
CFC-FREE
Sellotape
rotring 2000 isograph
STAEDTLER MARS-LUMOGRAPH
CLEAN COLOR
LUMOCOLOR 318
permanent
SUPERFINE
WINSOR & NEWTON MADE IN ENGLAND

For the time being we will only discuss the suitable supports for two-dimensional illustration. A smooth, pure white surface is by far the best for transparent mediums and the colours gain strength from the white base. Opaque mediums create a more solid layer, therefore a slightly textured support may help the paint to grip better.

Art board is usually made up of a layer of quality paper mounted onto a pulp base, and is produced specifically to maintain its smoothness, without separating or creasing, however wet the surface becomes. This is not the cheapest support, but some art boards are available with double sides which are ideal for beginners to experiment on.

CS10 board is the most popular and commonly used support for airbrushed work. There are very good reasons for this. It is totally smooth, so will not throw off any fibres, and the surface will hold its own against erasers, scraping back and low tack adhesives. Masking film will also adhere evenly to its hard flat surface, decreasing the risk of paint running or bleeding under the mask.

Bristol board is an alternative which differs in its make-up by the fact that it is a laminate and is available in different weights according to its number of layers. This has a slightly softer surface than CS10, but is still suitable for airbrush work, especially when a softer image, perhaps combined with brush work, is required.

Watercolour board has the same properties as CS10, but the surface is more textured. Although this makes masking more difficult — since it will not adhere completely flat to the surface — for an image which requires loose masking the textured surface will give the airbrushed artwork a more painted feel and add interest. Be warned though when removing masking or scratching back as the surface is very fibrous and can come away.

Do not be fooled by other boards that appear to have the same surface. Only these specific art boards are manufactured to withstand excessive dampening, and any other type will bubble and the surface layer separate from the base.

Papers are always a cheap alternative and although they cockle when damp, it is possible to stretch them over a solid board and secure with tape. This is obviously not suitable for a finished artwork, since any small creases will show when airbrushed, but definitely does the job while practising your control exercises.

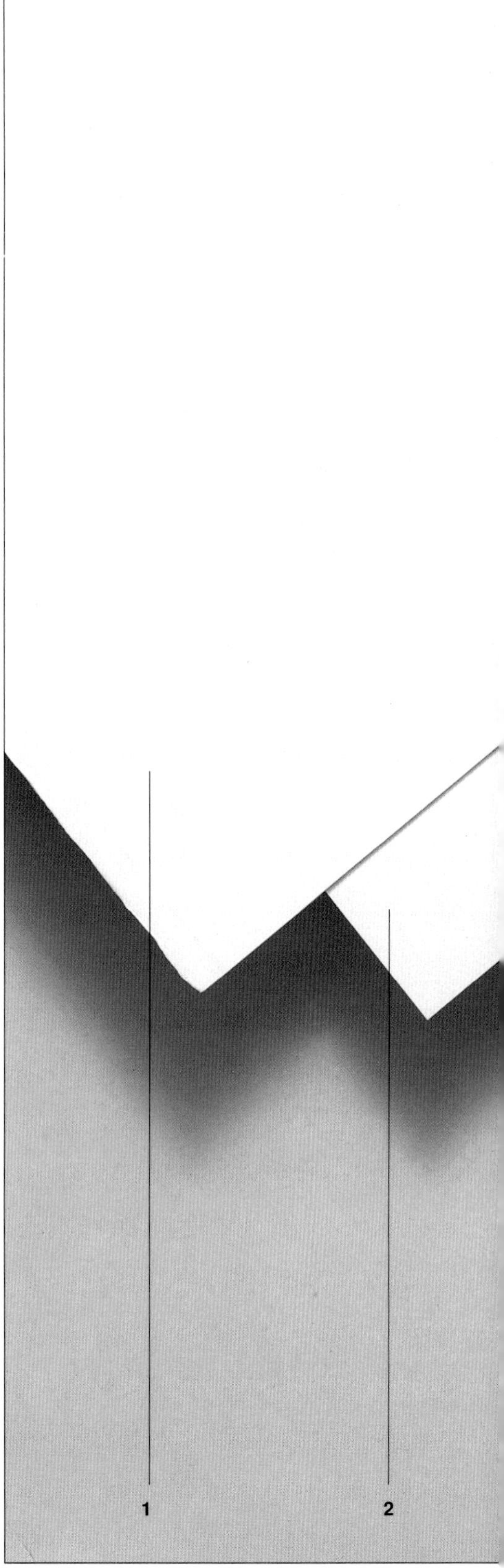

Left to right:
1, 2 & 3 Textured watercolour boards of varying weights.
4 & 5 Light and heavy weight CS10 board.
6 & 7 CS10 papers.
8 Bristol board.

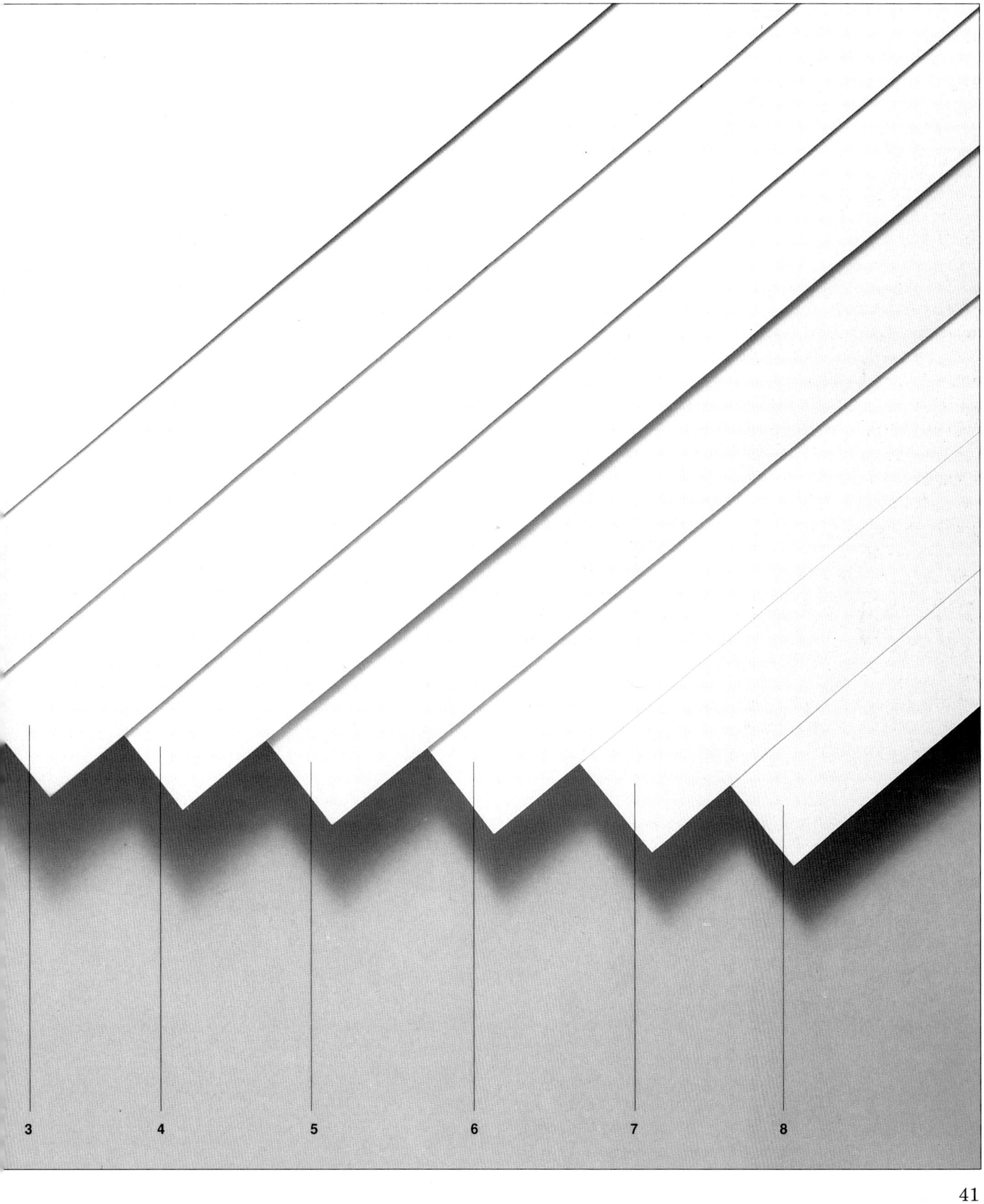
3
4
5
6
7
8

Basically any type of medium which can be mixed to the right consistency — that of milk — can be blown through an airbrush. However, some are far more suitable than others.

Inks are a favourite with airbrush artists because although they are transparent, the colours are very vibrant. They can also be bought already mixed to the right consistency for airbrush work. Having said this, the waterproof variety should be used with great care and never allowed to dry in your airbrush. So always flush your airbrush through immediately after use.

Watercolour has been long established as one of the most suitable mediums for airbrush work. It is water soluble which is a major bonus as this makes it easy to clean your airbrush after use. Although readily available in bottles already mixed, if your choice is to mix your own, always use distilled water. Its transparency allows the chosen colour to be built up gradually by over-spraying in layers. However, this does mean that you can only work from light to dark.

Gouache, like watercolour, is water soluble which makes it ideal for airbrush use as it can be flushed through so efficiently. The similarity ends there though as this is an opaque medium. The opacity is produced by the addition of precipitated chalks bonded with gum arabic. Gouache lays good solid colours, and because of this it is possible to over-spray dark colours with light totally successfully.

Acrylic would not usually be included as a suitable medium for airbrush work. It was really developed for large-scale paintings as it dries quickly, with a tough plastic finish which is almost indestructible. For this reason, flushing it through an airbrush can be tricky since any paint left behind clogs and could prove disastrous. These days an acrylic is available with a built-in drying retardant which allows more time for flushing through — so always make sure you buy the right type.

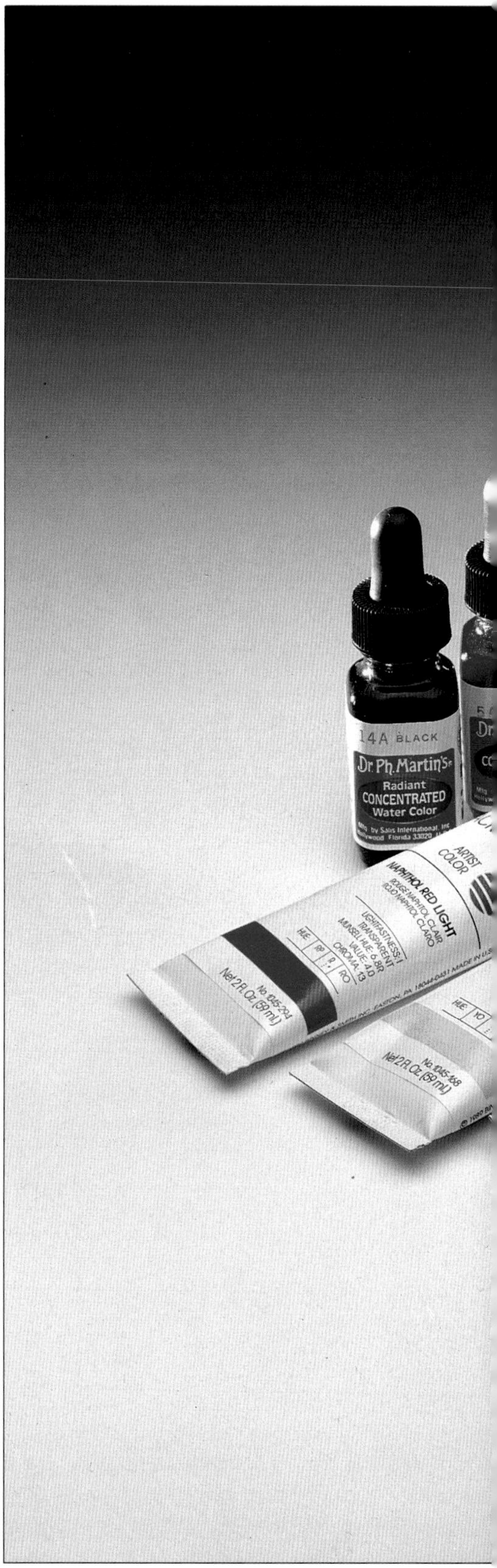

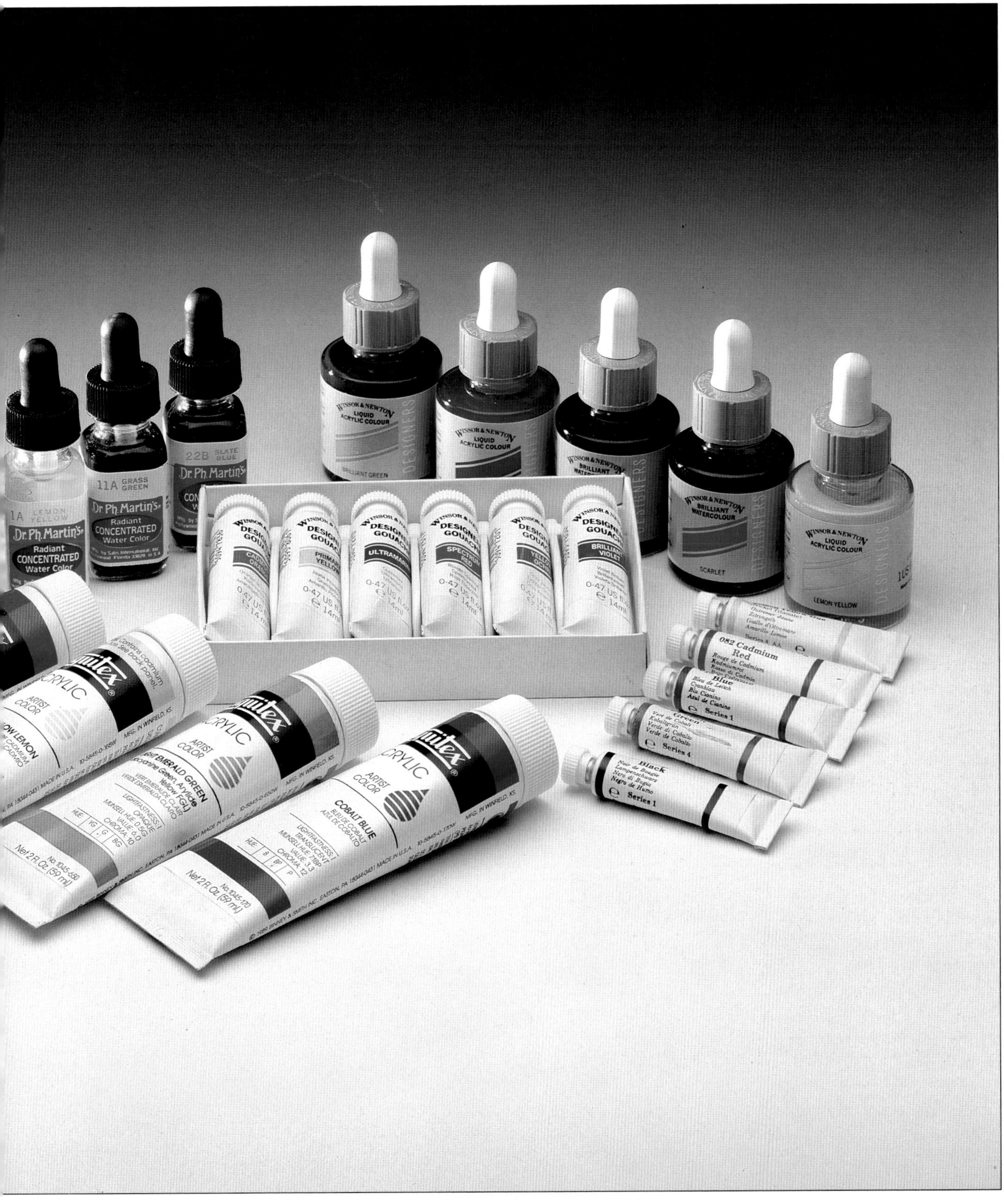
Dr.Ph.Martin's
Radiant
CONCENTRATED
Water Color
11A GRASS GREEN
22B SLATE BLUE
WINSOR & NEWTON
LIQUID
ACRYLIC COLOUR
BRILLIANT GREEN
DESIGNERS
BRILLIANT WATERCOLOUR
SCARLET
LEMON YELLOW
DESIGNERS GOUACHE
BRILLIANT VIOLET
0·47 US fl.oz
14ml
082 Cadmium Red
Rouge de Cadmium
Blue
Series 1
Series 4
Black
ACRYLIC
ARTIST COLOR
COBALT BLUE
Net 2 Fl. Oz. (59 ml)

If your chosen support is an art board the following procedure must be carried out, without fail, before you do anything else.

1 Make a wad of kitchen roll — so that you can hold it from the back — and pour on enough lighter fuel to dampen, not soak, it.

1

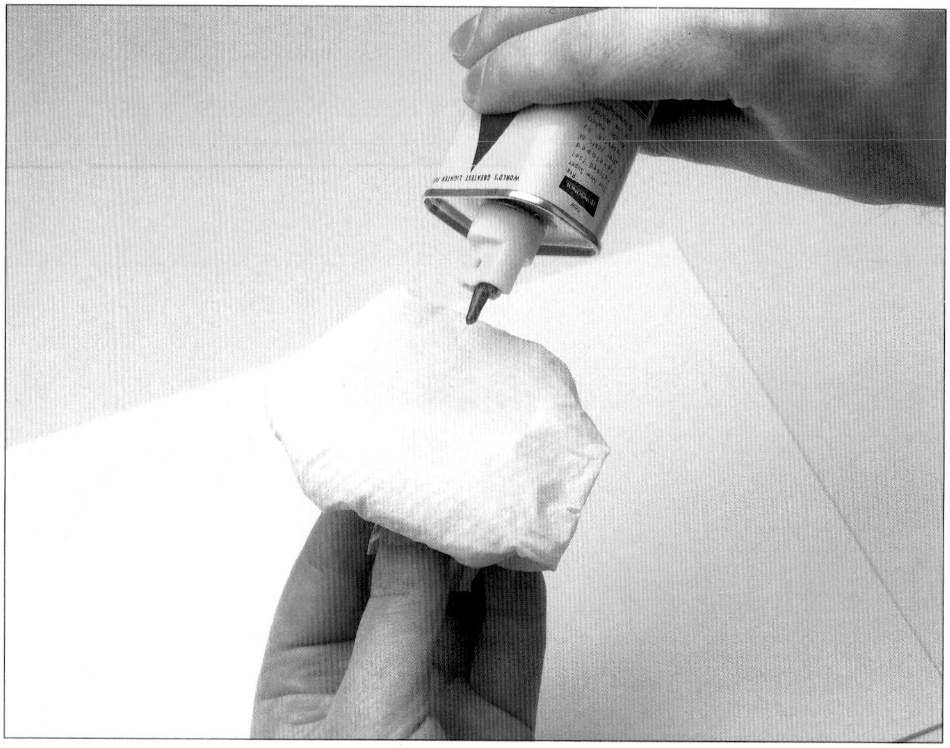

2 Applying light pressure, draw the wad carefully across the board making sure that you have covered the whole surface. This might seem unnecessary, but never be tempted to skip this preparatory stage. Marks can be lurking on the surface that might not even be visible. Apart from dust or grease, fingerprints are the biggest culprit, since once you have sprayed over a print it will show through clearly and you will never be able to get rid of it.

2

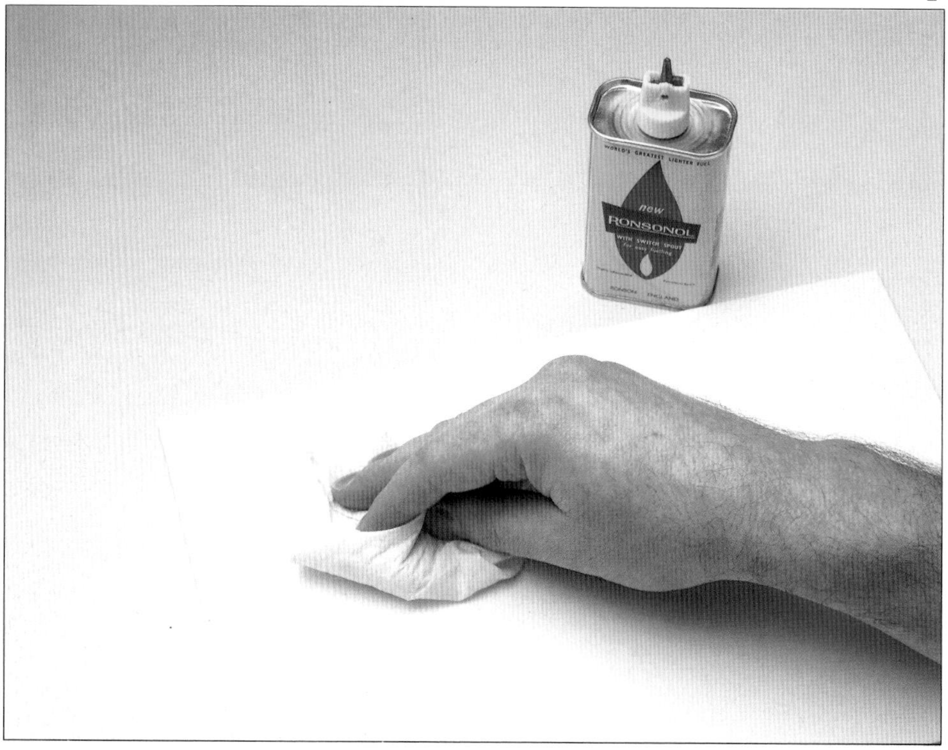

Under no circumstances do you want to work out your initial drawing for an artwork directly on your support — its just too expensive to risk mistakes on — so whether you are working freehand or from a reference it is important to learn how to transfer images quickly and cleanly. There are three main methods; scaling, using transtrace paper and direct image transfer, although I must say that with scaling I would suggest doing it onto a piece of paper first and then using transtrace or direct image to actually put it onto the support.

SCALING

If your initial reference is in the form of a photograph or a page from a book or magazine, but is not the right size, the grid technique is an ideal way to scale your image up or down.

Using a ruler and pencil draw an accurately squared grid over the top of the image. On a separate piece of paper draw another grid. The scale of your second grid will obviously depend on whether you are scaling up or down. Here the image is scaled up, therefore the grid squares are of a larger scale. On this you will then be able to plot your reference points by referring back to the original image.

TRANSTRACE PAPER

The initial drawing used here was created to a brief from one of the artist's clients. They were most specific regarding Nelson's eye patch, but through research for the reference it was discovered that Nelson never actually wore an eye patch! It was in fact a miniature screen suspended on an arm attached to the inside of his hat. This shows how sometimes you have to ignore the facts and be willing to employ a bit of licence to please your client.

1 Attach your initial drawing to the support with low tack masking tape. This is important as you will be able to remove it easily afterwards without damaging the surface of the board or ripping the paper.

2 & 3 Transtrace paper works on the same principle as carbon paper and is available in any colour. Sandwich a sheet between your support and the initial drawing, making sure that the coated side is face down.

1

2

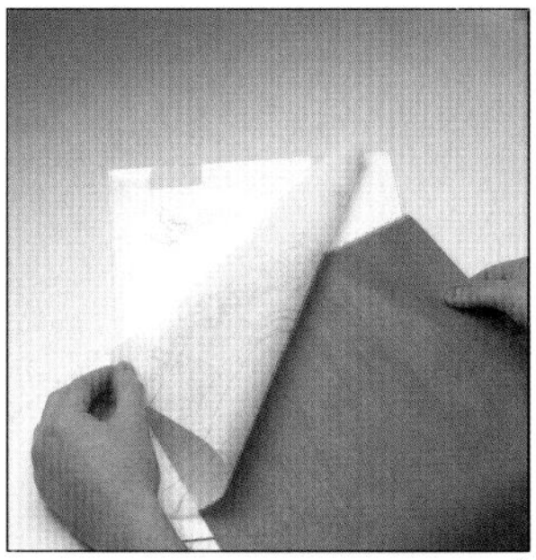

3

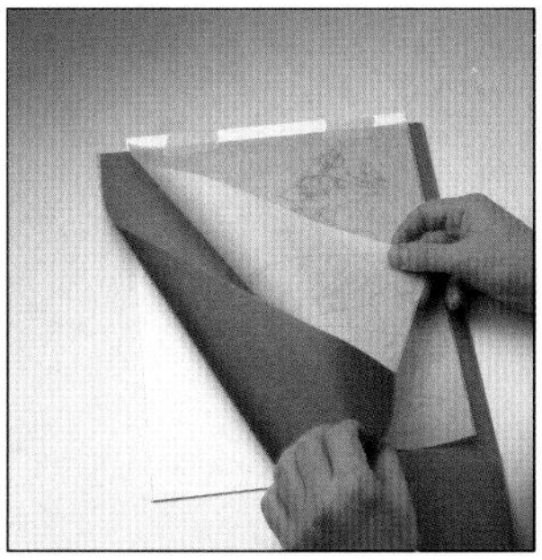

4

4 Start tracing carefully over your pencil drawing with even pressure, making sure that your top drawing is well secured so that there is no chance of it changing position. When you have completed this, peel back, the transtrace and your drawing will now be on the support.

This is a wonderfully quick method of transferring an image directly onto frisk, but is only suitable for single outline images such as lettering.

1 Using a soft pencil draw your chosen image onto a piece of board.

2 & 3 Peel the frisk away from its layer of backing paper and place it carefully over your initial drawing.

4 With a wad of kitchen paper or a soft cloth, smooth over the frisk applying a reasonable amount of pressure to make sure that there are no air bubbles.

1

2

3

4

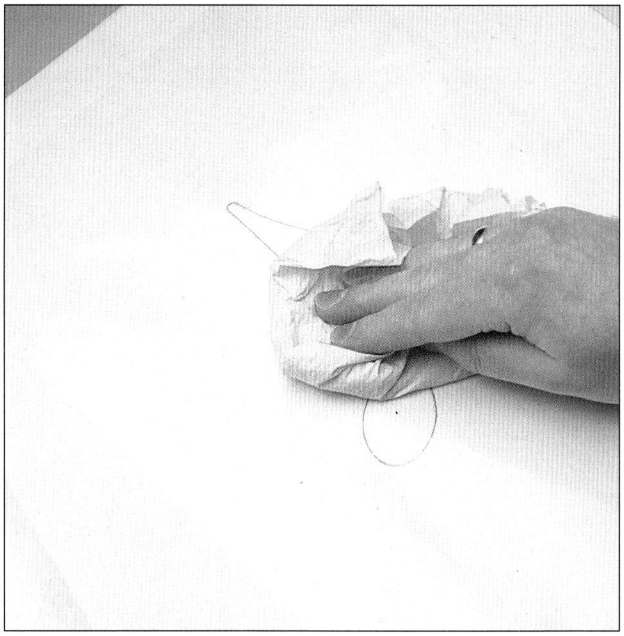

5 Burnish gently, following the pencil lines of your drawing. Although, as here, actual burnishers can be bought, any hard, rounded object will do the job just as well. For example you could well use the wrong end of a ballpoint pen or pencil.

6 Peel the frisk away from your drawing, and the image will have been transferred directly onto it.

7 Peel off the whole sheet of frisk and carefully re-lay it onto your support.

8 You can now cut around the image with a sharp scalpel, thereby creating an instant mask.

5

6

7

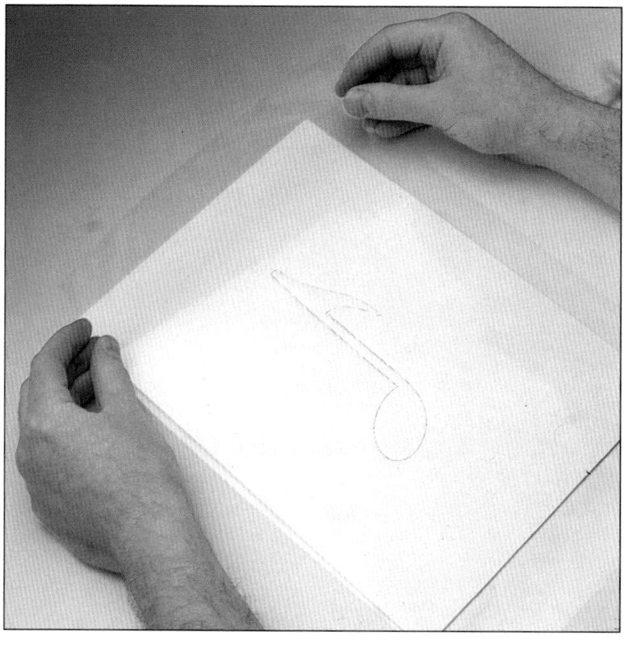

8

There is one more thing before you finally start to use your airbrush, and that concerns the sort of images that you should be thinking about creating. the beauty with airbrushing is that there are no limits. I cannot think of a single style, texture, object or living thing which the airbrush is not capable of rendering. So in this area you have total 'carte blanche'. Whether your flare is of a technical nature, naturalistic, abstract, landscape, or even if you just want to add personal touches to your decor, the airbrush is the tool for you. In the picture, I just collected objects from around the house, shells and pebbles found on the beach, books, pictures ... you name it, the airbrush can do it!

RT NOUVEAU

Chapter 4

In control

By the very nature of the title of this chapter, that is exactly what you are going to aim to be. If there was one simple and quick answer to becoming a successful airbrush artist it is patience. Being able to control an instrument or fine tool can be compared to learning to ride a bike. You keep on practising and yet you still wobble all over the road and often fall over. Then suddenly you are away and there is no looking back. It is purely to do with confidence and once you have gained that with your airbrush you will be in control. Whatever your artistic ability you really will be able to master the technique, and however you choose to apply it you should get a lot of fun out of it. Just persevere, and as you follow through the projects in this book you will soon realise that the art of airbrushing depends on control.

Throughout the projects in this chapter you may well think that the techniques are repetitive — but therein lies the key. Through learning a few basic techniques the end results can be of an extremely high quality and obtained in a reasonably short time. Do not mess about, but make a start right now, because you can and will crack it.

In control

LINE CONTROL

This exercise is to show you how just by altering the distance of the airbrush from the support you can change the end result from the spray. Whatever route your airbrushing takes in the future, you can be assured that your control over this distance will always be of the utmost importance in your work.

1 Holding your airbrush very close to the support, spray an even straight line. Although this exercise does not depend on the line being straight, it is good to practise this anyway, and, in fact, if you really do have problems you can always give yourself some help by running your airbrush along a ruler. By holding the airbrush really close to the support you will get a very thin, dense line.

2 Spray a second line, this time holding the airbrush about an inch (2-3 cm) above the support. Try to keep the airbrush at an even distance, since any up or down movement will show in the width of your line. The aim is to achieve a regulated line — this depends not only on the height of the airbrush, but also on keeping an even finger pressure on the trigger of your airbrush. As you may discover, this is in reality much harder than it sounds.

3 Your third line should be sprayed with the airbrush held a couple of inches (5 cm) above your support. As you can see that this will give you a much broader line with the spray quite diffused. Make sure that you get into the habit of starting your sweep before you operate the spray.

4 You can now repeat this exercise doing line after line on the same support, gradually increasing the height of the airbrush for each sprayed line. It is vital that you start and stop spraying each line while still moving the airbrush or you will get a thick blob of paint at each end of it. Carry on with this exercise until you are totally satisfied with your results.

1

2

3

4

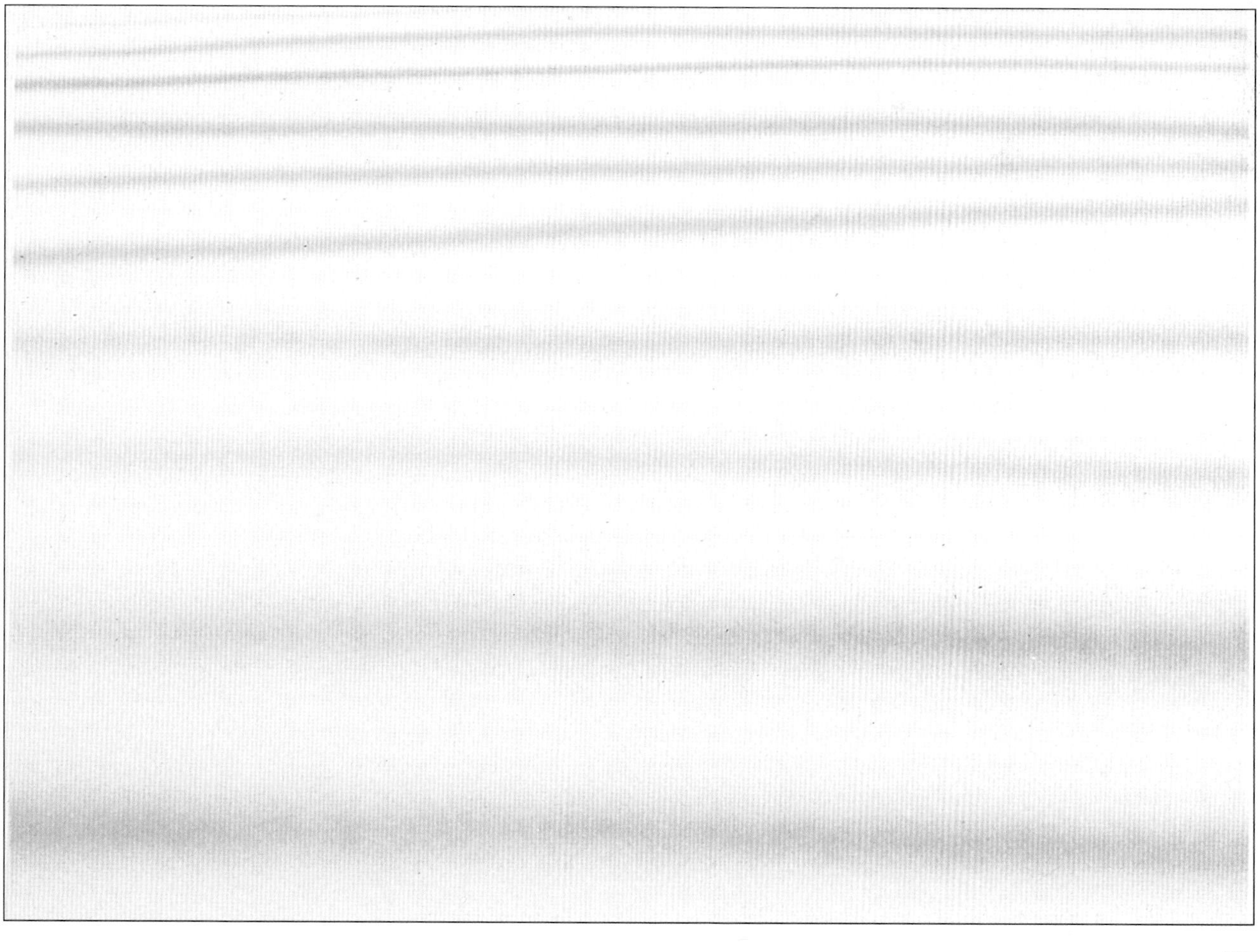

Next to line control, gradation will be your most useful technique to learn — an effect unique to airbrushing. A handy hint before you begin is never to spray for too long. A minute amount of paint will build up in the inside rim of the nozzle when you have been spraying the same area for some time. Eventually this will form into a tiny droplet and will be blown onto your artwork creating a blob of paint. To avoid this, stop every now and again, and spray onto a piece of scrap

1 First cover your support with frisk, then cut a rectangle in the middle of the frisk and peel this off. Spray horizontal lines, either freehand or using a ruler for guidance, to make a gradated band of colour across the top edge of the rectangle. Make sure that the paint overlaps both edges of the box in the same gradated colour — neither tailing off nor getting stronger.

2 Continue spraying this area to strengthen the gradation of colour from solid at the top to nonexistent about one third of the way down the box. You may find it helpful to cover the lower part of the box with a scrap of paper to prevent any accidental overspray. Spray in complete horizontal lines, starting with the darkest area at the top and gradually holding the airbrush further back from the support for the lighter tones at the bottom.

3 This process is now repeated for the bottom of the rectangle. If you are nervous about spoiling the top half, wait until it is dry and cover it with a piece of paper. Spray a few horizontal lines across the very bottom of the box, again making sure that you continue past the edges.

1

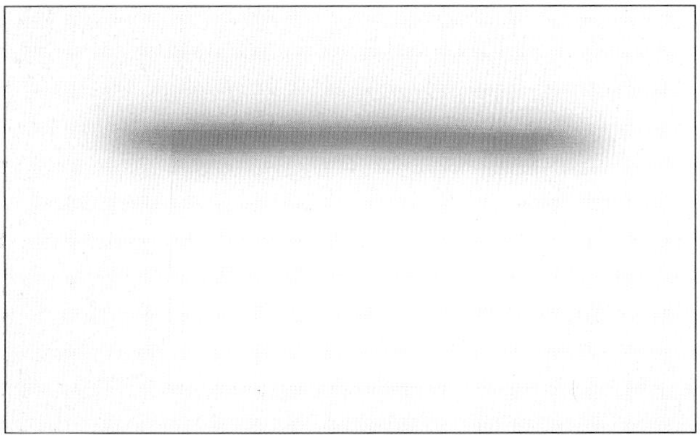

2

3

4

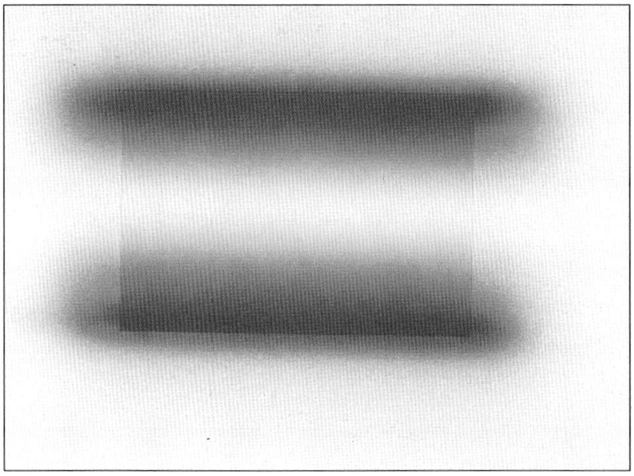

4 Build up your gradation with further lines of spray, pulling back for lighter lines towards the centre of the box. You may well wonder why it is necessary to work in such a small box when you could easily work direct onto your support. By using a mask you lose the start and end of each line which can often be messy and you therefore achieve a beautifully crisp outline. Not only this, but in practice you will often be spraying gradated tones inside very small masks, and so it is best to get into this way of working as quickly as possible.

5

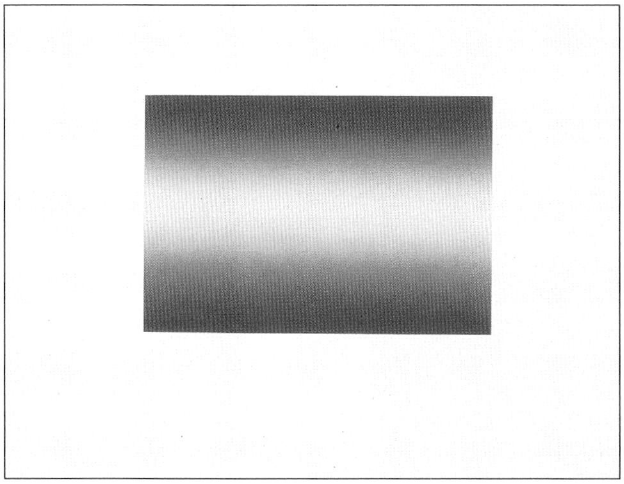

5 Once the paint is dry you can remove the frisk to expose your finished, gradated box. The gentle change of colour from dark to light to dark has been achieved solely by your control of the airbrush. Gradation is a fundamental technique for airbrushing and so it is worthwhile repeatedly practising this exercise until you are totally happy with your results.

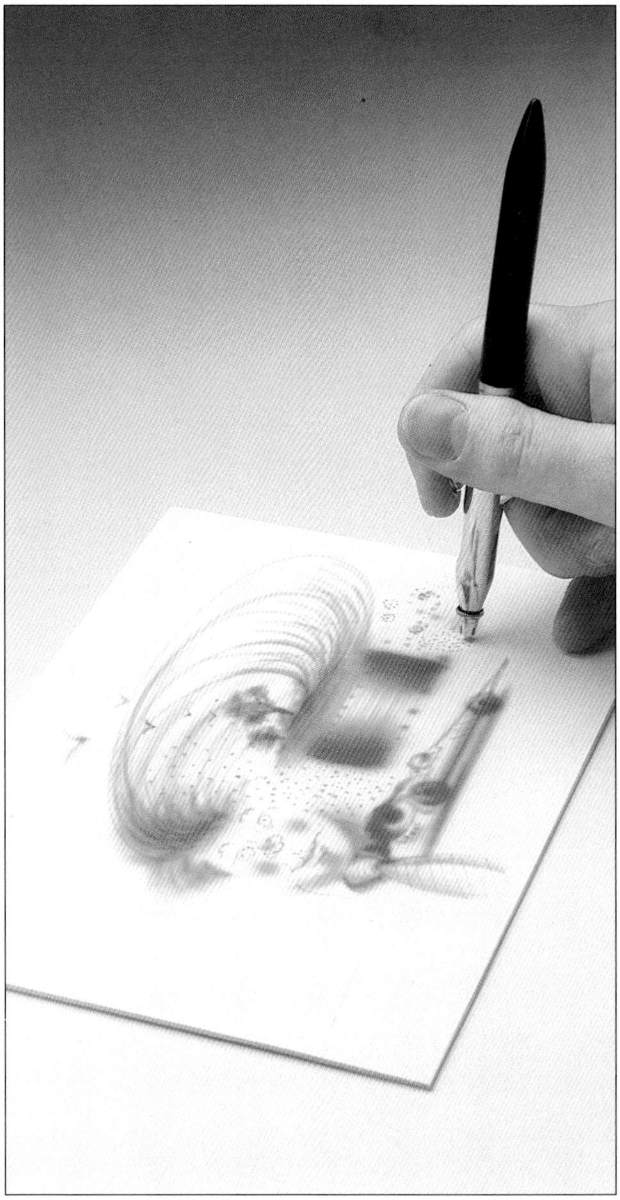

Although in the previous control exercises we have talked about confining yourselves to a preset area, freehand spraying must also be learnt. It is all part of building up your confidence and really getting the feel for airbrushing. Just take a piece of card and experiment, for example, with quick bursts at varying distances from the support. As you can see here, tiny pin head dots are rendered by holding the airbrush just above the support. This proves how the airbrush is capable of creating fine detail. Try sweeping actions, swirls, lines, arcs and circles — just relax and aim!

Virtually anything that is used to block out an area of an image, thereby preventing any medium touching the surface underneath, can be called a mask. Masking is as important as mastering the control of your airbrush. It can make or break your finished artwork, and like Laurel and Hardy, one is never any good without the other. There are two main categories of masking — loose and hard.

Loose masking is when the mask does not necessarily touch the surface of the artwork or is resting loosely on the surface, allowing a certain amount of spray to fall underneath its edge. Although the outline will still be there, the feel will be much softer. Hard masking, on the other hand, will give a very definite, crisp outline and is always attached to the surface of the support, the aim being not to allow any spray to spread underneath it.

Loose masking covers the broadest spectrum, as you will see from the special effects shown later on these pages, but even a hard mask can metamorphose into a loose mask simply by holding it above the surface. Creativity stands much more of a chance within this category, so experimentation and your imagination can be put to full use.

Hard masking is much more regimented, and although various materials can be employed in this category — such as card or templates — by far the most common material is frisk. This wonderful material, which was developed especially for airbrushing, supplies the perfect hard mask and holds all the qualities necessary for any intricate details. It is available in sheets or rolls and is completely transparent. There is a backing sheet which, when peeled off, reveals a low-tack surface which will adhere to the support yet not damage the artwork when removed. You can even lay it over areas already sprayed in the full confidence that it will not even slightly lift any paint from the surface. Just one point to remember. though — the sprayed area must be completely dry. The latest version is matt, the only advantage being that you can draw directly onto its surface. The most important rules with frisk are: to always make sure that there are no air bubbles, and when cutting it a fresh scalpel blade must be used to ensure a clean line.

Perhaps one should mention one other type of masking — liquid. This is a rubber solution which you paint directly onto the surface of the support. Its plus side is that it is excellent for tiny details where cutting a mask is tricky. In theory all you do is peel it off afterwards. However, on the minus side it can lift fibres from the surface and leave a slightly yellowish tinge. If you do opt to use this type of masking, do a test run with it first on your chosen support.

Although acetate has not been mentioned, before frisk arrived on the scene it was the most popular form of masking. It is similar in that it is transparent, which is vital when working on a complicated artwork. The drawback of acetate is that it has to be weighted down to keep it flat on the surface. This is a problem with intricate areas, and if accidentally knocked it can take ages to re-align. On the positive side, acetate is still a very useful form of mask since it can be easily moved and can be used as a loose mask.

1

1 Laying your frisk correctly is the most important part of any project which involves frisk masking. After your initial image is on the support, always give the whole area one final wipe with lighter fuel. Although you might find this removes some of the pencil lines an indentation in the surface of your support will always remain.

2

2 Peel off approximately the first two inches (5 cm) of backing from the frisk and lay this over the bottom of your support. Take a metal rule, and with the side edge gently lay the frisk. Working from the bottom upwards, smooth the frisk down, pulling the backing paper off as you go. Although this can be done with a cloth, this method will make you one hundred per cent sure of completely removing any air bubbles. Never discard the backing paper. Being greaseproof it will prove invaluable to place pieces of mask on which will need to be reused during a project, or for placing over the artwork to rest your hand on when adding any finishing touches.

It has never ceased to amaze me how many extraordinary and bizarre effects can be achieved through masking. Absolutely anything can be used. All the examples over the following pages were created by everyday objects, but by using a little imagination anything is possible.

1 In this exercise you are going to create a quick background of dreamy mountains. Take a sheet of paper and tear it roughly into a shape which represents a mountainous contour. Place this approximately a third of the way up from the bottom of the support, and weight it down with coins. You do not have to be too thorough as the edges should be quite soft. Spray fairly densely around the mask, grading down towards the bottom of the support.

1

2 Now tear a second piece of paper, making the 'mountain' contours a different shape. Place this above the first outline, again weighting it down. Spray around the edges — but do not build up such a dense tone — grading down to the 'peaks' of the first mountains.

3 Tear your final 'mountain range' from the paper and repeat the process, spraying in an even lighter tone to simulate the feel of misty mountains in the background. Remove the mask to reveal a complete mountain range. *See illustration 4*

2

3

4

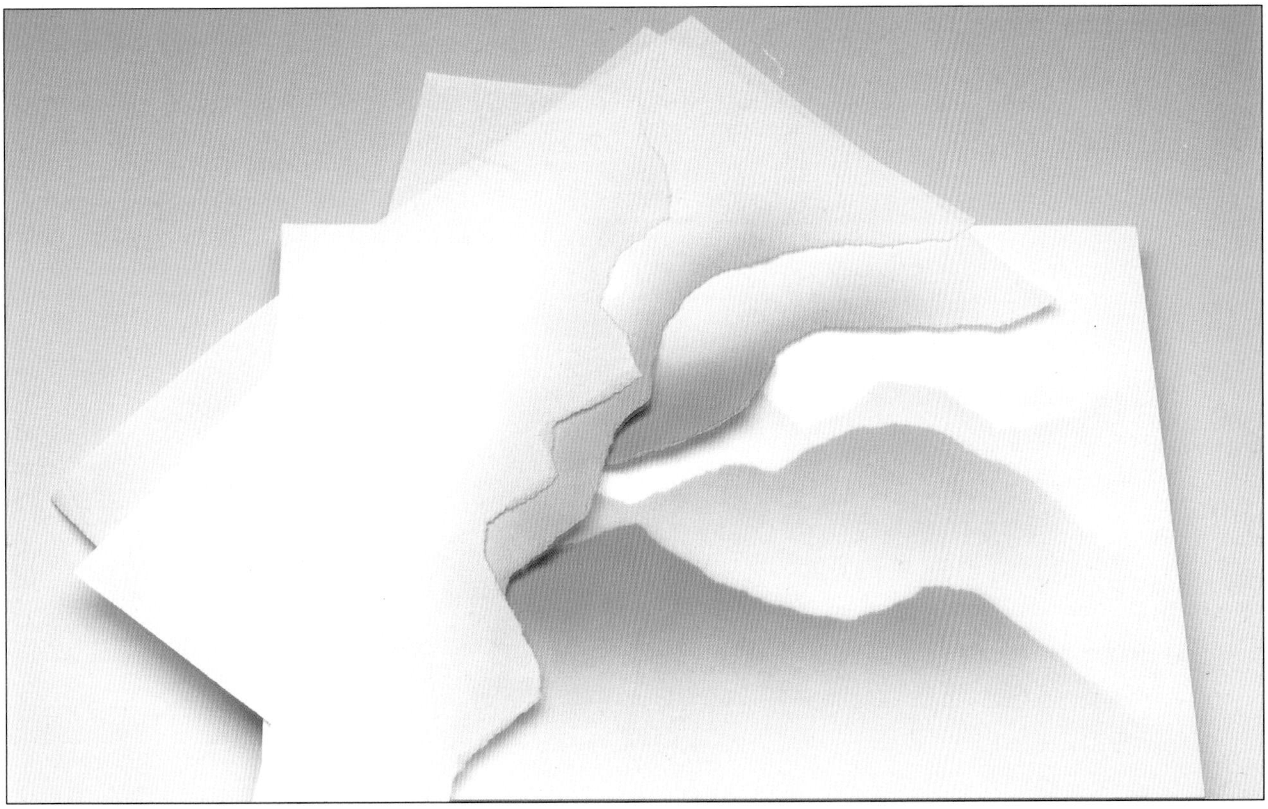

Coins
Throw what's left of your grant (if you are a student) or overdraft at random onto a support and spray over. Shake the support slightly and spray again. This process can be repeated as many times as you like until you are happy with the result.

Paper Clips
This was just an experiment, but the result ended up looking quite surreal, so we decided to show it! Another reason was to prove the point that literally anything can be used as a mask. You will never know what effect you will achieve until you actually give it a go.

Rope
I must say that this was one of my favourites, even the rope itself looked amazing after being sprayed! However, your aim is to create unusual results on the support, and by separating out the strands and spraying, the outcome is similar to the branches of a tree blowing in the wind.

Net Curtain
An off-cut from a net curtain has been laid loosely over the support and sprayed through. Although the effect is not exactly mind blowing, it has still created an interesting texture.

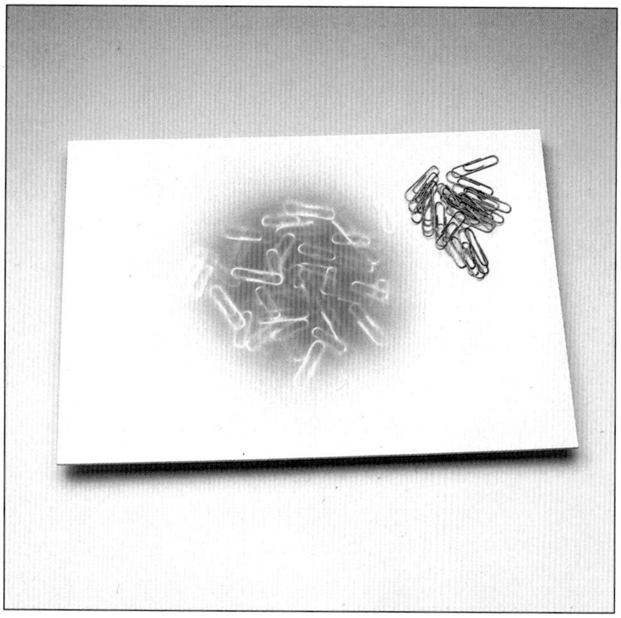

Rug Backing
This scrap of material would normally be found in a rug making kit, but continuing in the mood of nothing ventured, nothing gained, it was sprayed over. As you would probably be able to visualise the end result in advance, instead of laying it flat, try bending it in to slight waves. This minor alteration has changed the regularity, creating a far more abstract finish.

Leaves
Leaves give you the most incredible choice of shapes, and even if you do not use them as masks, the outlines can also be traced to make perfect stencils or patterns. However you are creating masks here, so take a variety of leaves and just spray round them, moving them across the support at random — as above — or in a regular manner. With all the different varieties of leaves around you the effects are infinite, so allow yourself plenty of time for experimentation.

One of the most remarkable aspects of airbrushing is the astonishing range of effects that can be so easily achieved. As you will see over the following pages the same basic shape can be made to look like glass, wood or chrome with very little effort. The list of textures and effects is in fact endless, and could well provide you with months of delightful experimentation.

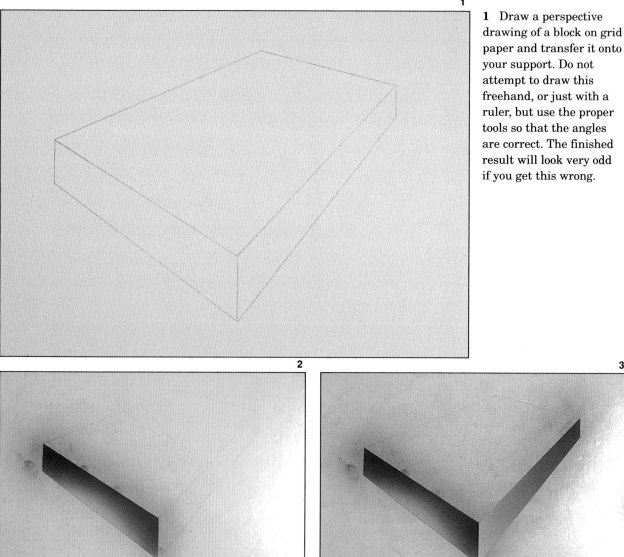

1

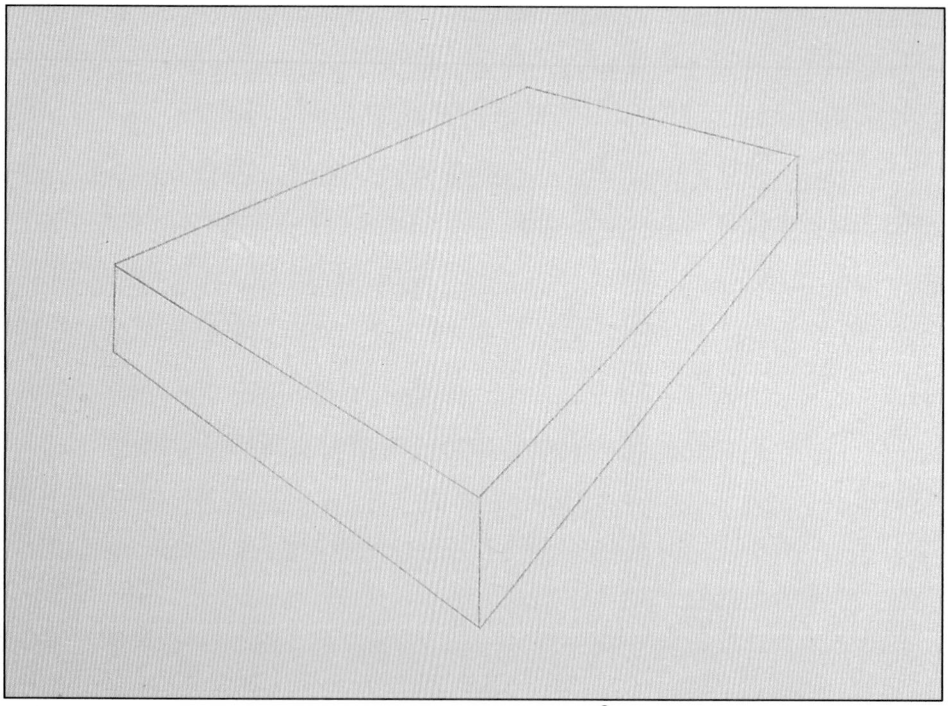

1 Draw a perspective drawing of a block on grid paper and transfer it onto your support. Do not attempt to draw this freehand, or just with a ruler, but use the proper tools so that the angles are correct. The finished result will look very odd if you get this wrong.

2

3

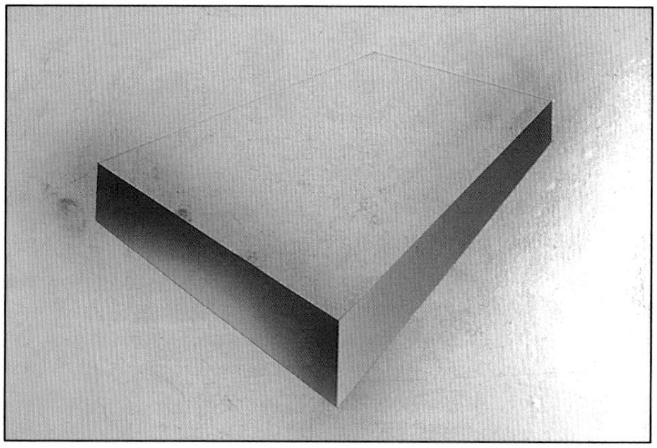

2 Cover your support with a layer of frisk and diligently cut along all the lines with a sharp scalpel. You want to start spraying on the darkest area first since any later over-spray of a lighter colour will not show. The front end is going to be the darkest, so peel off the frisk in this area to expose the support. Spray over this area with any colour of your choice since, as this is a plain effect, the colour is irrelevant. Do not lay a flat colour because the finished result will look much better if you gradate the colour from dark at the top and ends to light at the centre bottom.

3 Expose the second darkest area — the side of the block — and again spray over with your chosen colour. Spray gradually darker towards the back since this will help to give your image depth.

4 The frisk covering the third and final area can now be removed. You again want to spray this area darker at the back, with almost no spraying at all towards the front. Once you have finished spraying remove all the remaining frisk to expose the finished result. Note the stark contrast between the dark front and the almost pure white top. It is really important to achieve this gradation of colour within each area. Although the image would still have a three-dimensional look if you had just sprayed flat colour slightly lighter at each step (and you could well try this to see the difference), it is the gradation within each area and the contrast of one pair against another which ultimately makes this plain image work.

4

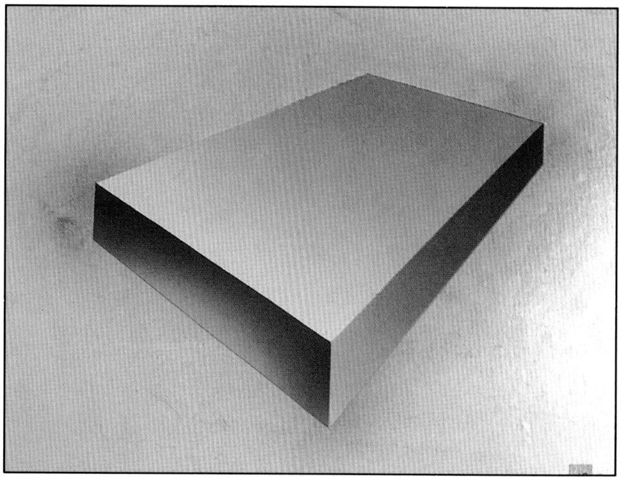

1

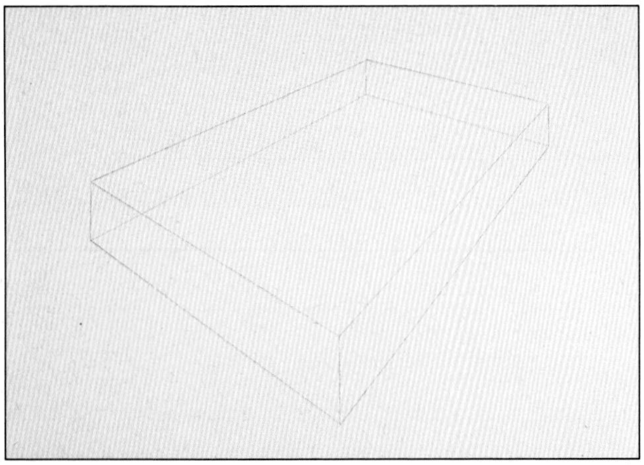

2

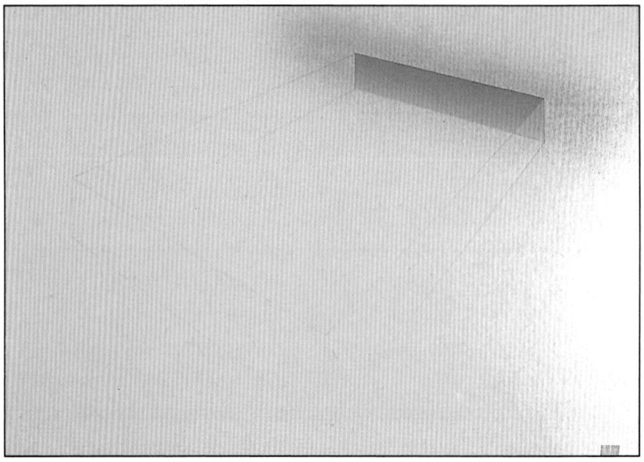

3

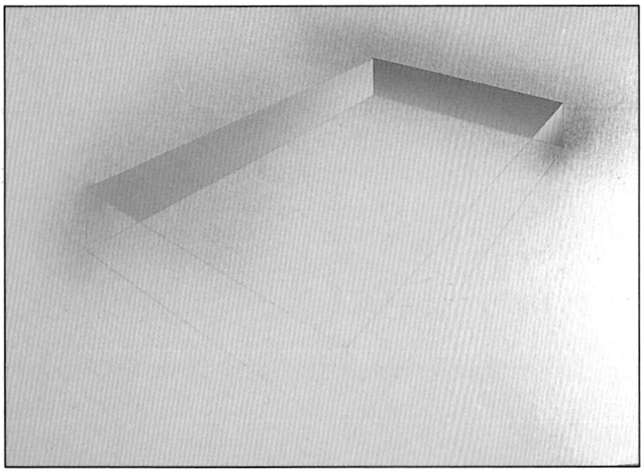

1 The beauty of practising on a basic shape like this block is that, once you have your initial drawing, it is easy and quick to keep tracing your basic image. However, this time it is important to show all six sides clearly.

2 Cutting the masks will be slightly more tricky for this exercise, so it will be better to do each section as you go along. Cut the back section first but not the whole thing, leaving the corner section where the side overlaps. Spraying in any colour of transparent medium, grade the tone to get lighter at the bottom.

3 The left side of the block can now be cut — this time leaving the corner where the front section overlaps. Spray carefully, building up the tone towards the front.

4 Your front section can be cut as a whole, and here you can see clearly how the overlap will give you more of a three-dimensional look now that this section of masking has been removed. Spray the whole of the front section, grading the tone again to be darker at the right corner.

4

5

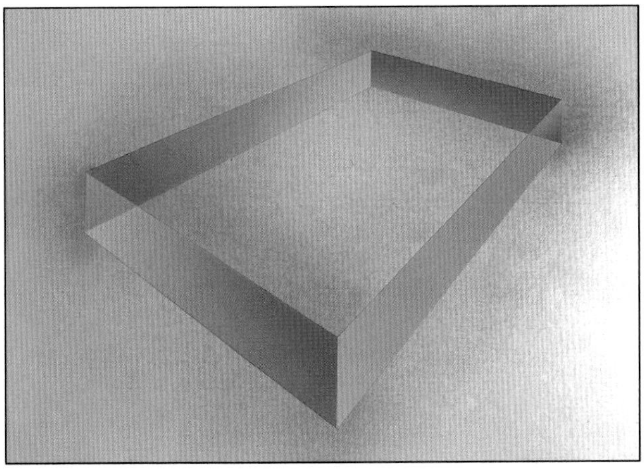

6

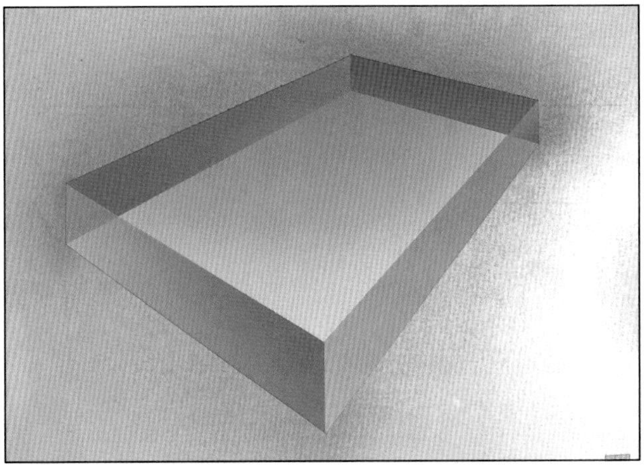

5 Cut along the whole of the right side and remove the mask. Using the same grading technique spray along the side, building up subtly towards the back.

6 Finally cut and remove the last top section of masking. Lightly spray over the whole of the block, allowing the white surface of the card to shine through. This will also overspray all the gradated tones previously created and darken up the corners creating a transparent, yet three-dimensional, image. Remove the remains of the frisk to expose your finished image.

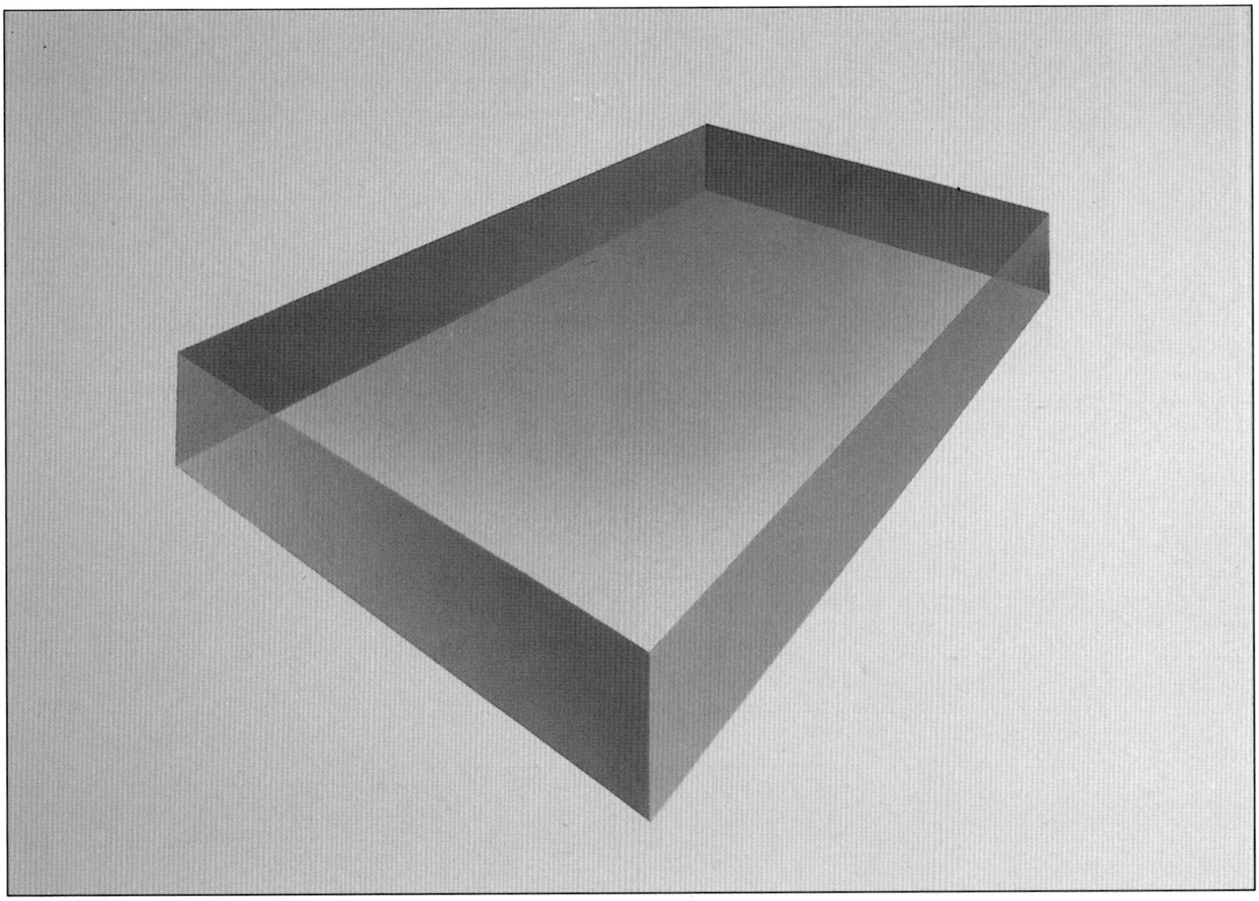

1

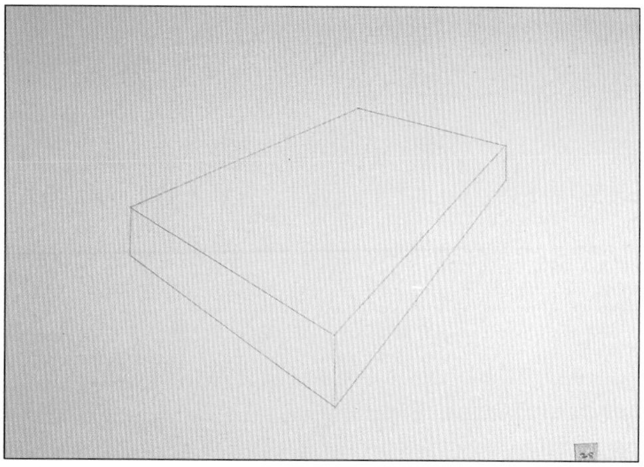

1 As you already have drawn your basic block all you need to do is trace it again onto your board.

2 With a fine brush paint in your wood grain in Vandyke brown. Do the top surface first and then bring the ends of your lines straight down the front end of the box. Although a knot-hole will add interest, be careful not to put in too much detail.

2

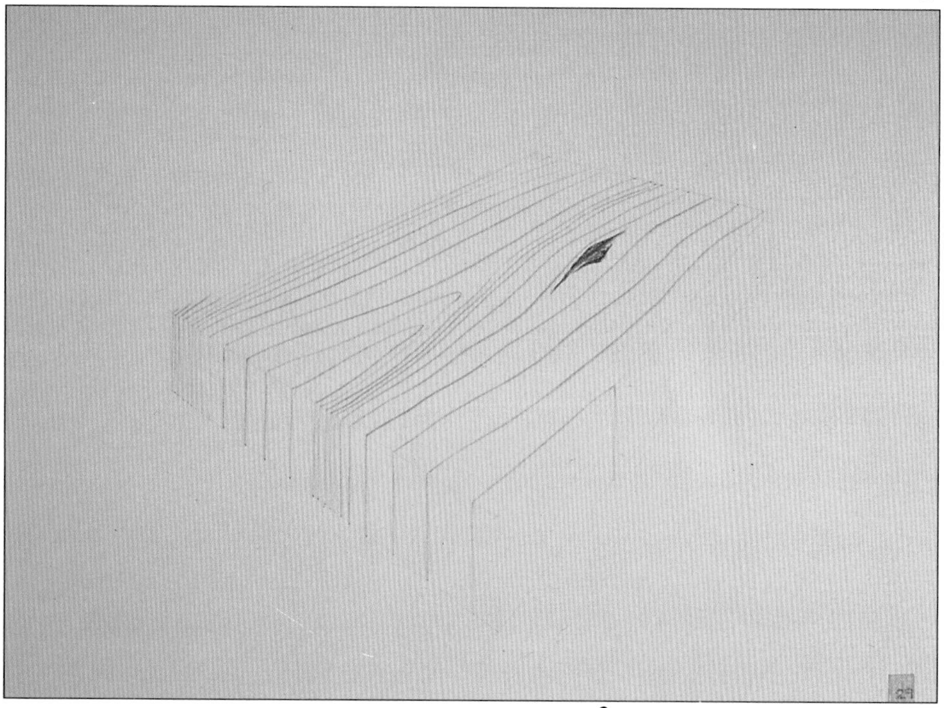

3 Lay down a covering of frisk and proceed to cut along the lines of the block. Do not cut along the wood grain lines you have just painted. Remove the frisk from the front end of the block and spray it with a mixture of brown and yellow ochre. Over-spray along your painted grain lines to give a 'woody' look.

4 Peel back and remove the frisk from the side edge of the block, and spray over with the same mixture of paint, again over-spraying the line of wood grain.

3

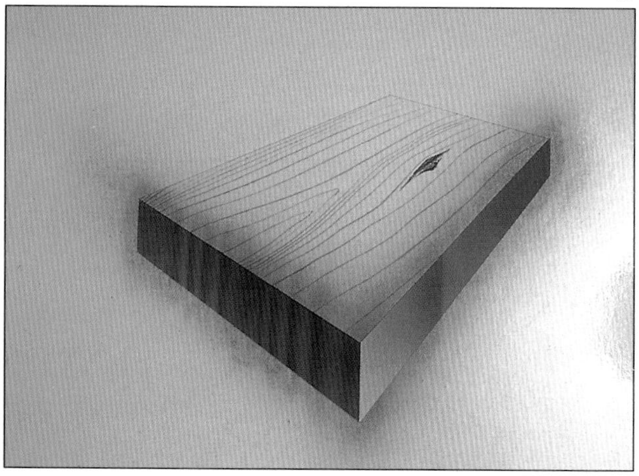

4

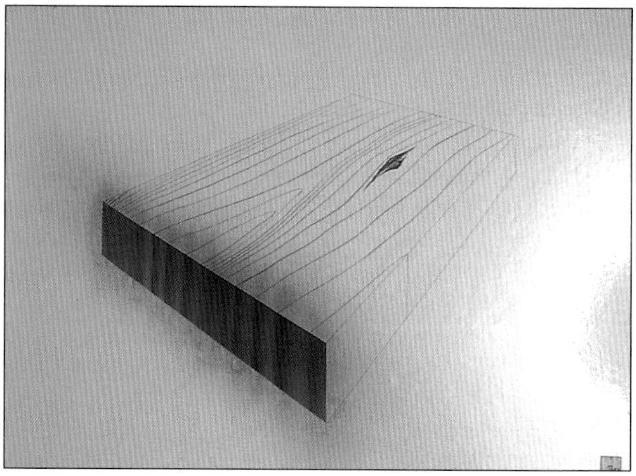

5

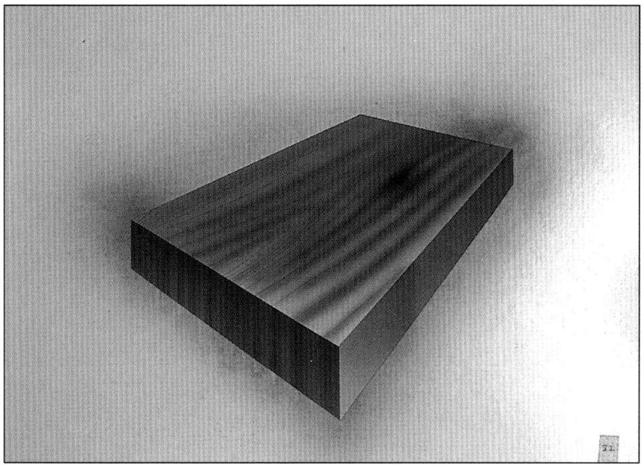

6

5 Expose the third and last area, and spray using exactly the same technique as for your first two areas.

6 The top of your block is obviously the largest area and will therefore be the point to which the human eye will be drawn first, so more detail can be added. Include highlights by scratching along the lines with a scalpel and reinforcing with a fine brush to give a more realistic look to the wood.

1

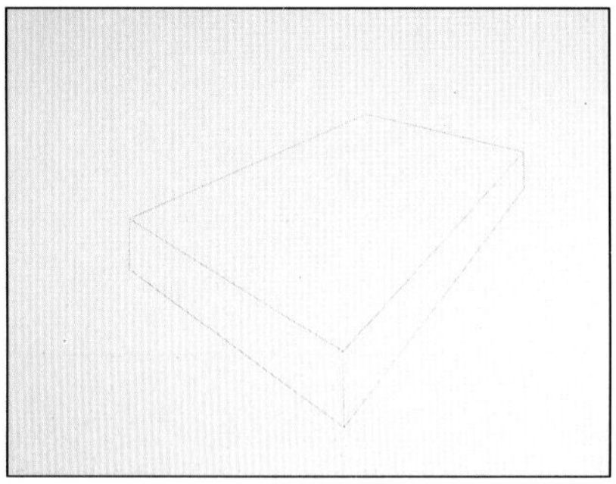

2

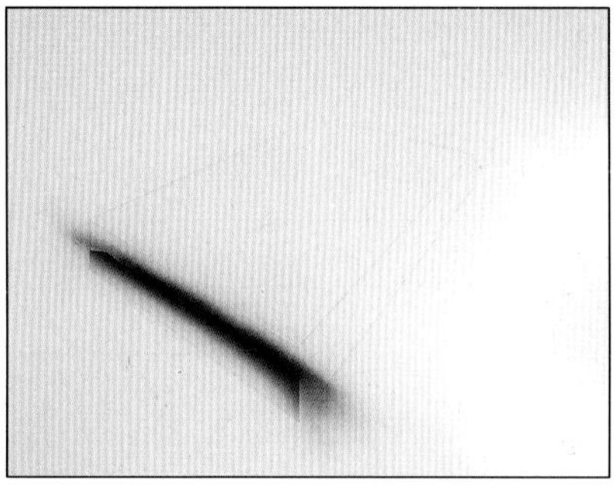

3

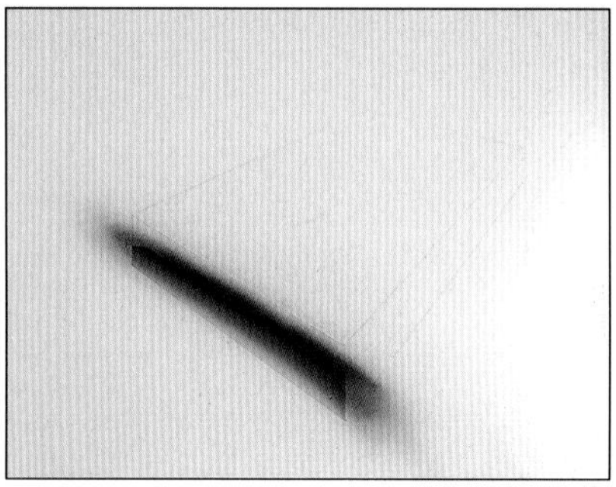

4

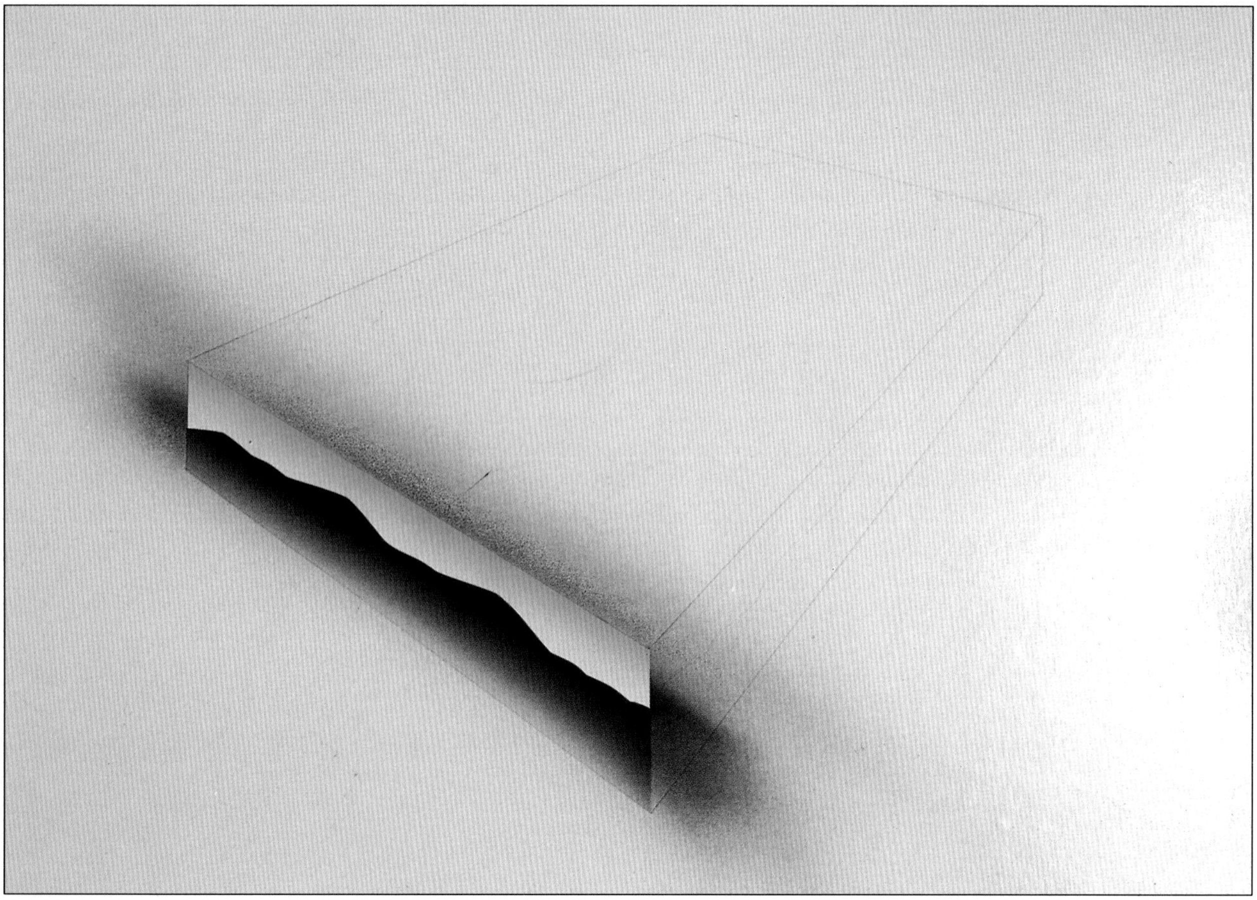

1 Transfer the block onto your support. In this exercise you are going to re-create a chrome effect. There is not really a true chrome finish as chrome is a reflective surface and therefore is nearly always shown throwing some form of reflection. In this instance it has been rendered by including an horizon line with reflections that simulate earth and sky.

2 Cover the image with frisk and cut along all the lines of the block. On your first section, about halfway down, make another cut — this time make a freehand 'wavy' line to denote the 'horizon'. Remove the bottom 'earth' mask and spray along the line with sepia.

3 Change the colour to a mix of red and yellow ochre, and fill in the rest of the section. It should be second nature now to remember to flush your airbrush through between each colour change.

4 Now remove the top half of the mask and spray in the blue 'sky', keeping it lighter towards the 'horizon' line.

5

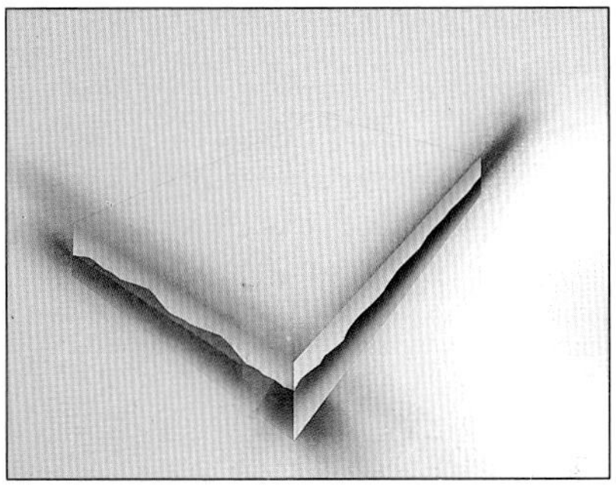

6

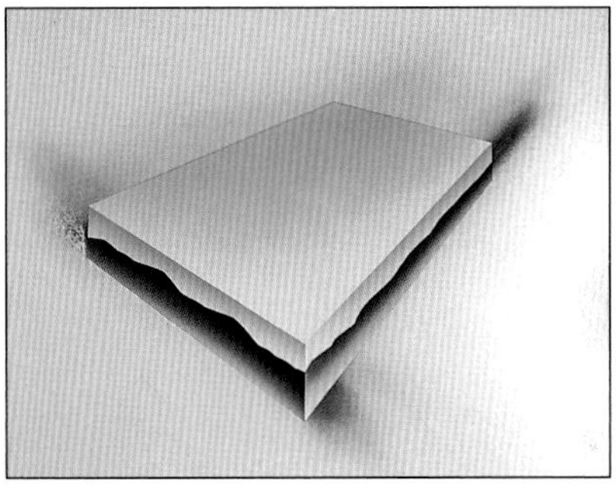

7

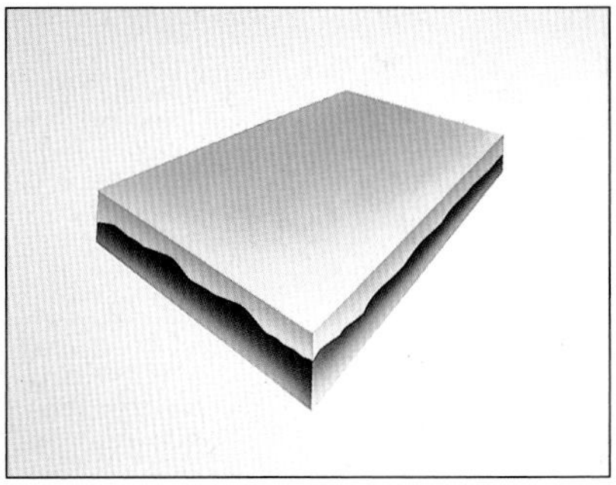

5 Before starting along the side of the block, re-mask the whole of the front section. Repeat the process of spraying the lower section in sepia, changing to a mix of red and yellow ochre. Remove the upper part of the mask and spray in the blue.

6 Your final area can now be exposed and sprayed in blue, making the spray much lighter towards the edges.

7 Remove any remaining masks from your support. Although your work may look finished there is still one more essential step. The final touches to really capture the impression of chrome are the highlights. Scratch gently along the edges of the block with a scalpel to reveal the support and add definition. Using diluted opaque white, spray a freehand burst on the corner and halfway along the front edge to create the effect of shiny metal.

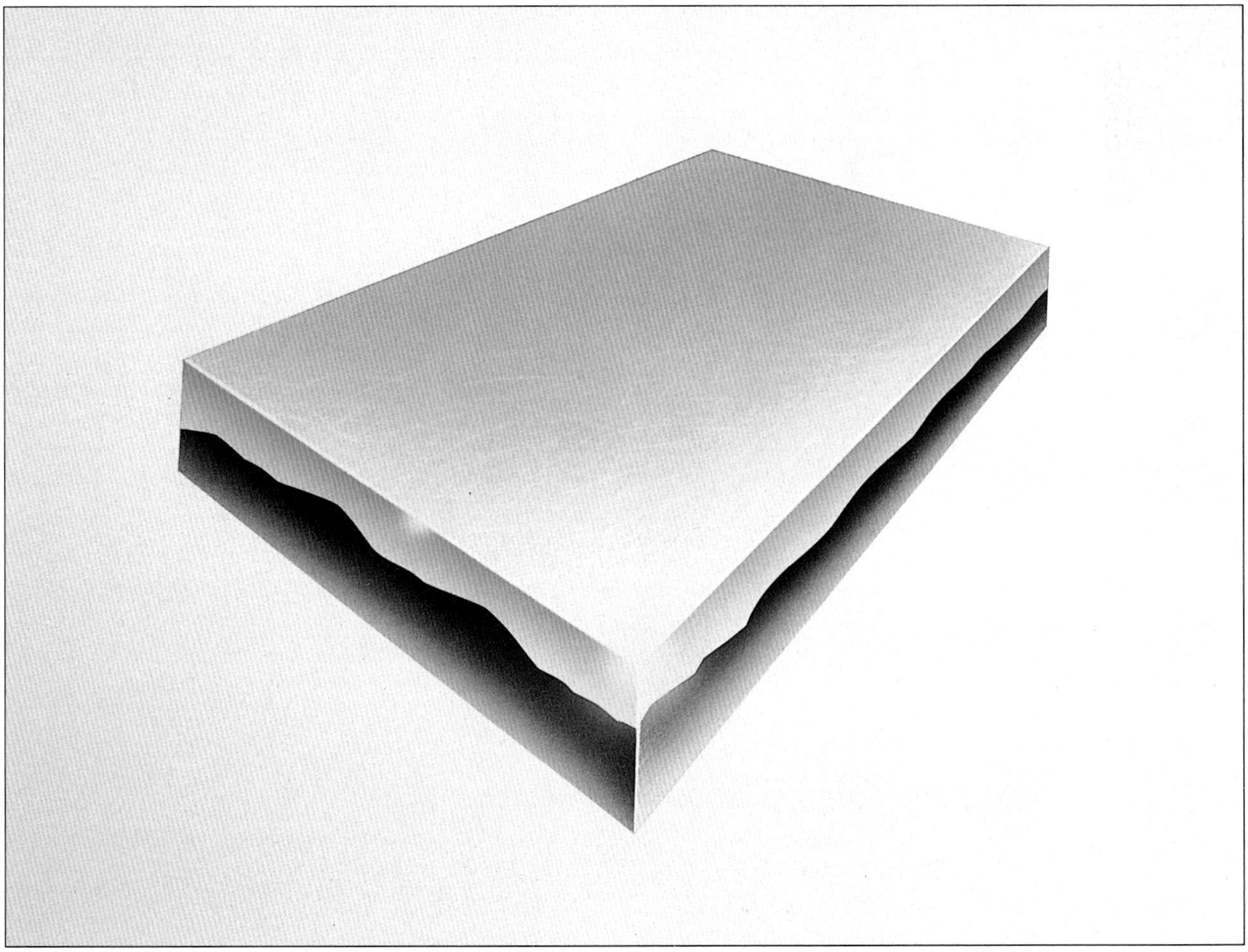

Having just been shown a range — albeit small — of surfaces that the airbrush is capable of creating, here are a variety of surfaces that you can spray onto. There are a whole range of specialist paints available that have been developed specifically for certain surfaces, such as glass and fabric, but it is nearly always worth a telephone call to the manufacturers — if your local art suppliers cannot help — as they will have all the necessary information. So 'no holds barred', as well as depicting anything, you can literally spray on anything you like.

Here you can see how, just by creating one stencil, you can customise a whole range of furniture. In this case a plain kitchen cupboard has been transformed. One stencil was cut, based on a zebra skin, and sprayed through. The stencil was then turned round and held over the other door. You do not have to stop there, the same stencil can be placed over the backs of chairs, or even on the front of your fridge.

This image was scaled up from a photograph found in a magazine, and cut into a huge stencil. This was then bravely sprayed directly onto to the wall. Although only one colour has been used, the impact it creates on first entering the room is sensational to say the least.

Simplicity can often create some of the most stunning effects, and this classic image of palm trees works perfectly for this front door. A stencil of a tree was made, but in this case the actual palm tree shape that was cut out was secured over each glass panel in turn and sprayed around, leaving the shape clear. This looks particularly striking at night when all the house lights are turned on, and the whole image becomes beautifully illuminated.

As you can see from the trees and fence in the background, this is much bigger than life size. Its final destination was the outside of an American style restaurant, hence the large scale. The image was sprayed directly onto a sheet of hardboard and then cut out with a jigsaw. When spraying to such immense proportions a lot of freehand work is used, as the definition does not have to be so precise.

Although it is possible to spray directly onto leather, if you have spent a fortune on a jacket, this might not be such a good idea. A separate piece of leather was used, and the image sprayed onto it. The outline shape was then cut out and stitched onto the jacket, to avoid any costly accidents.

No one would expect an individual to use this technique, but as it is a concept, who knows, this could well be the 'poster' of the twenty-first century. Just think of the scope for advertisers. Basically the image is sprayed onto the equivalent of a light box, which, when illuminated, not only gives the artwork a life of its own, but shows every minute detail, right down to the reflections in the chrome and on the paintwork of the car.

Believe it or not this image is a small part of the biggest airbrushed artwork in the world. The completed mural — which contained nearly a hundred individual characters, as well as the hieroglyphics in the background — was 650 feet long, and was a hoarding around a building site in London's docklands. It was unveiled by the Minister for Arts, and won the artist a very prestigious award.

Chapter 5

Gradation

If you have been working hard and relentlessly practising all the exercises in Chapter 4, you should be feeling much more confident and at ease with your airbrush. If, on the other hand, you are in total despair, don't give up. The saying that practice makes perfect really does apply to the technique of airbrushing.

Once you have mastered the art of gradation you will be amazed at the wide range of effects that can be achieved. Again, as with all airbrushing techniques, it is possible to master as long as you keep at it. A simple background of one colour moving through from dark to light, showing all its various tones, can look stunning. Basically your main aim with this technique is to be able to blend one colour or tone into another by almost imperceptible degrees. Nine times out of ten you will use this skill as an integral part of your artwork.

In the project described over the following pages you will find out for yourself, that the stark, moody image was created by a process based purely and simply on gradation.

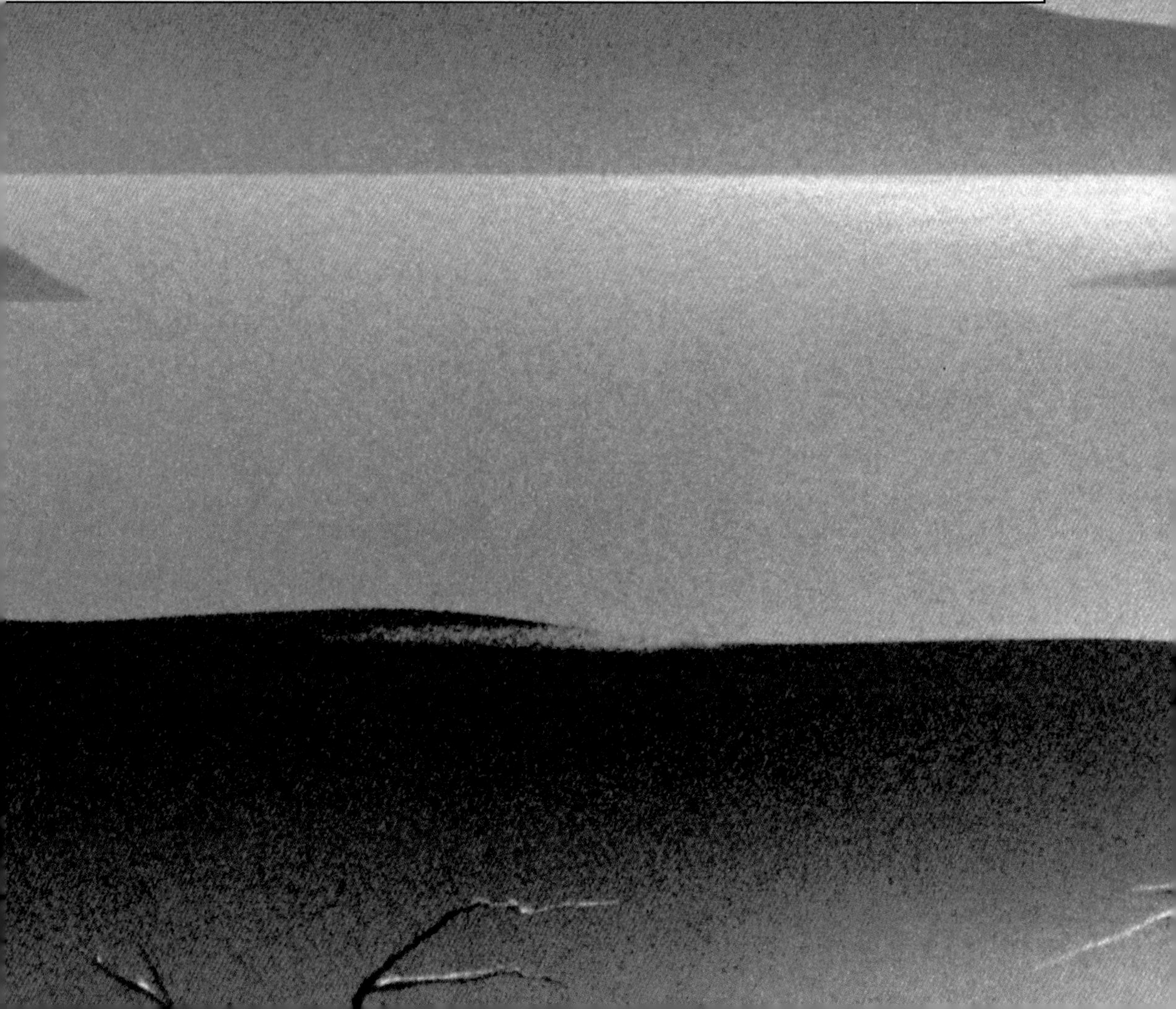

Gradation

CREATING A BACKGROUND

1 Before you start any composition always do an initial rough sketch showing the layout and the dark and light areas so that you can get a feel for what the finished artwork will look like and to enable you to plan your masks. Keep it handy so that at any stage you can refer back to it to remind you what colour or shade should come next.

1

2 From your sketch make a line drawing showing the edges of all your masks to come.

3 This line drawing can now be transferred with the aid of transtrace to your support, which in this case was CS10 board.

4 Cover your line drawing with a sheet of frisk and proceed carefully to cut along all the lines with a sharp blade. Take your time and make sure that you do a good job as this will be the key to a successful end result.

5 Remove the masking from the darkest areas first — the tree and its reflection in the water. In most cases you will be working from dark to light, since every time you remove another segment of your mask you will be over-spraying sections already done and so making them darker and darker. Do not attempt to cut out the thinnest branches of the tree as it is much easier to add these at a later stage with a fine brush. Cover the exposed area with a spray of Payne's grey mixed with a dash of Cobalt blue.

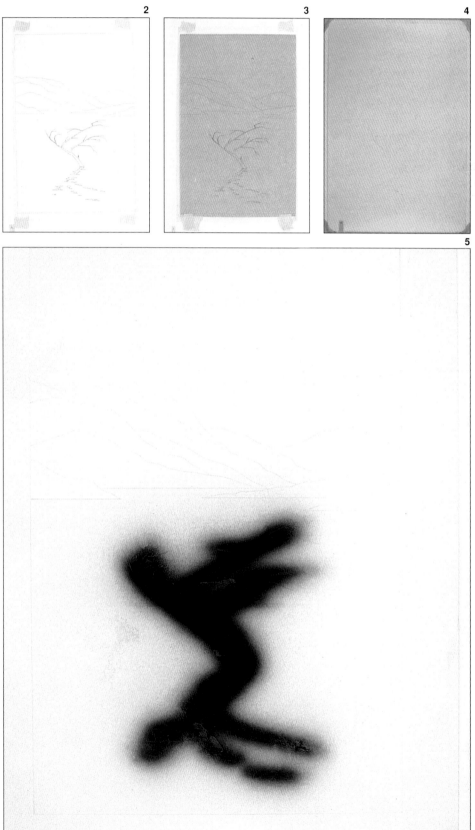

2

3

4

5

6 In this composition the hills become lighter in the distance, so start by removing the mask for the small hill at the front and spraying over with your colour mix. Then continue by removing the masks for the two hills one step back and spraying slightly lighter over the exposed areas.

7 This process is repeated in steps, working towards the faint hills at the back, removing the next lightest areas and spraying more softly at each step. Don't try to hurry this process up by removing too many masks at once, have patience and proceed slowly to achieve the best effect.

8 Finally you arrive at the very lightest hills for which you only spray just a hint of colour, leaving the support almost showing through. You will see that your picture now has a lovely depth to it due to the gradation of colour from front to back.

9 You can now remove the mask covering the sky and spray over with your mix of Payne's grey and Cobalt blue. Try not to lay down a heavy, flat colour, but rather gradate it from top to bottom as this will greatly enhance the finished appeal of your work. Make sure you do not allow the sky to become too dark.

6

7

8

9

10 Cover the whole top of your artwork to prevent any accidental spraying while you concentrate on the water at the bottom. Before you start on that, though, this is an ideal point at which to add the thin branches to your tree with a fine brush. The effect of water in this case is best achieved by lightly spraying freehand with the same colour mixture as before, but this time dilute it partially with water. Build up the tone with several sweeps of your airbrush.

11 The building up of the water tone is a gradual process and should not be rushed. It could well be worthwhile to practise on a scrap of paper until you feel confident enough to spray onto your masterpiece in the making.

10

11

12

13

12 Continue spraying freehand over the area to build up tone and create ripples until you are satisfied with the effect you have achieved. Do not be tempted into over-working this area, since if the tone gets too dark it could ruin your picture.

13 Remove the masking from the central area of your artwork, and with a scalpel blade gently scrape the edges to soften them. You can then very lightly spray this area. Finally, add highlights to the branches of your tree by carefully scratching off the paint with a scalpel blade so that the white board shows through.

Chapter 6

Photo-retouching

Photo-retouching is one of those areas that people seldom even realise exists, but in fact nearly every photographic advert in a glossy magazine has been retouched in some form or another. This alone should help you to understand just how good professional retouchers actually are — indeed the level of skill and control required is often far higher than that for illustration. But don't despair, the basics of photo-retouching are really easy to pick up.

Although you may have no desire to become a professional photo-retoucher on no account should you skip this chapter because the techniques over the following pages apply to all areas of airbrushing and need not be restricted to photographs. In addition, the truth of the matter is that for the beginner photo-retouching does at least get you away from the 'blank paper' syndrome and can often provide enough inspiration to really get you going.

You can rummage through the attic, find an old black-and-white picture of your mother, and give it to her as a lovely gift. Alternatively, you can let your imagination run wild by adding whatever takes your fancy to the holiday snaps — the sky's the limit so enjoy yourself, because that is what photo-retouching is all about.

Photo-retouching

TINTED PORTRAIT

One of the first uses of the airbrush was for colouring early photographs, and this use still goes on today, although for different reasons. The primary use of colour tinting nowadays is when a client wants a colour photograph, but only has a black and white shot available, and therefore an entirely natural style of tinting is required. Getting away from the professional world though, colouring your own old black and white shots is immensely satisfying and can often bring these forgotten pictures to life. Remember that whenever you are working with photographs always have more than one print made, as this allows for experimentation and accidents. Although dry mounting the prints first is always a good idea, it is especially important for colour tinting. As with any process which involves excess dampening of the support, this will prevent the surface bubbling or cockling. For this project watercolour paint was used throughout.

1

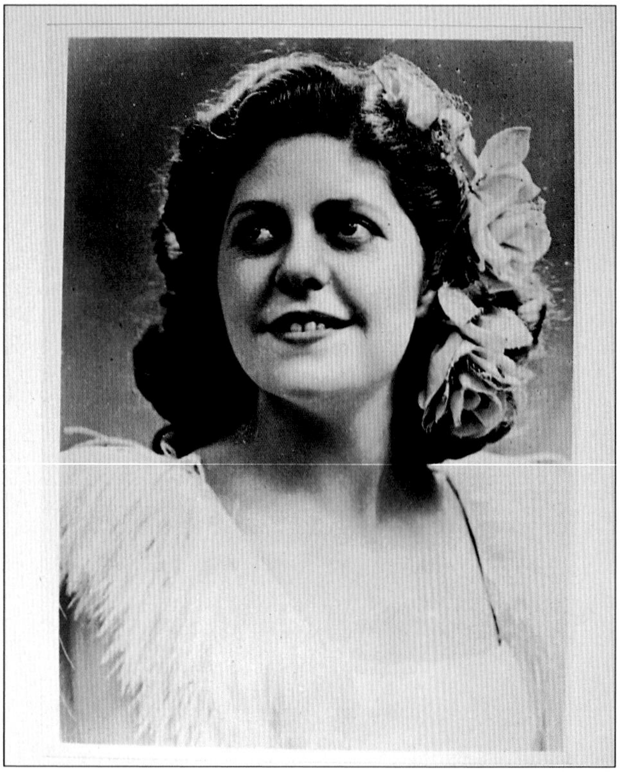

2

3

4

5

1 Dry mounting is not expensive and will provide you with a perfect surface for colour retouching.

2 Cover the whole image with frisk and cut around the outline to expose the background. Then spray this with the darkest shade which is a mixture of Hooker's green and Ultramarine.

3 The next area to spray is the hair. As you cut the mask try not to make the edge too hard as this could end up making the hair look like a solid wig. Spray this area with warm sepia.

4 The lips will be one of the trickiest parts, and a fresh blade in your scalpel would be helpful here as even the tip needs to be razor sharp for lifting such a tiny mask. Make sure that you leave the teeth covered. Any deep red shade would be suitable for the lips, but here scarlet was chosen.

5 The whole of the face and flesh areas are now unmasked except for the eyes and teeth. Skin tones are always difficult, so to achieve the right mix of colours it is wise to test your combination out first on a scrap of paper. As this was a black and white photograph the area was already quite dark and so a blend of permanent red and yellow ochre gives the right effect.

6

6 It is now safe to remove the tiny mask covering the teeth, although this could in fact be left to the final stage. The dress is next to be exposed and sprayed, and although transparent yellow was used here, any colour of your choice would be fine so long as you bear in mind that you want to be working from dark to light. The reason for this is that any over-spray of pale watercolour will not affect the darker shades.

7

7 The area of masking over the flowers is now removed and sprayed to match the dress. Remove the remaining masks, not forgetting the eyes. Any other finishing touches can now be made — blue for the eyes and then a transparent permanent red tint over the cheeks.

COMPOSITION CORRECTION *FOOTBALLER*

The most classic mistake when taking photographs is a total lack of regard for composition. How many times have you taken what you thought was a perfect picture, only to find that, once developed, an insignificant item in the background — that you hadn't even noticed — has totally ruined it. Although sometimes a source of amusement, in reality this can often be a huge disappointment. Retouching the backgrounds on photographs with an airbrush is perfect for covering up errors in composition, as this example shows. In addition, you can use the techniques employed here not only to correct pictures, but also to enhance portrait shots by 'knocking back' the background so that the figure really stands out, or for creating gentle vignettes to get a soft, dreamy image. It is far easier than you would guess, and well worth a go.

1 This Brazilian footballer, Carlos Alberto, seems to be sprouting a tree from the top of his head. The aim here is to hide the tree by spraying over it with the background colour. You should never work on your original photograph since accidents can easily happen. So get a copy made and then dry mount that onto a piece of board.

2 Cover the print with a layer of frisk and then carefully cut out around the figure. The more time and care you spend on doing this the better, as the quality of your end result will depend on how good your mask was.

1

2

3

3 The next stage is gradually to spray across the background at the top, in this case with an opaque white, until the image of the tree can no longer be seen even under an intense light.

4 Gently peel off the layer of frisk to see the finished result — with no exotic hair-style — from which a new print can be taken.

In the previous two exercises we have covered the main areas with which professional retouching is involved. A much less common application, although arguably immensely more fun, is that of adding items to photographs to create surreal or amusing images. The techniques employed here closely follow those used in any normal airbrush work, and so are ideal for the beginner who may be terrified by the idea of working with photographs. In this example the artist was looking through his holiday snaps when he found a sky view which was crying out for a 1950s American 'B-movie' flying saucer to be added. So have a rummage through your photo albums and let your imagination run wild.

1

1 Once you have selected the photo you want to use, have a couple of large prints made of it. If things go to plan you won't need to use the second print, but it is always better to be safe than sorry. As you are going to be spraying onto this print, for your own convenience it is best to get the largest print possible to give you plenty of 'elbow room'. Dry mount your print onto a piece of board.

2

2 Roughly fix down a piece of tracing paper over the print, and follow in pencil the outlines of the various elements of the picture. You do not have to be incredibly precise with this, as you are only going to be using this as a guide to where the flying saucer will sit on the photograph.

3 Remove the sheet of tracing paper and tape it down on an piece bit of card. You can then draw your flying saucer straight onto this. Note how the artist here has used faint centre lines to make sure that the flying saucer is visually correct. As this drawing is the basis from which you will be spraying, make sure that you take your time, and that you are totally happy with it before you go any further.

4 Since this is a simple image, the quickest way of copying it onto frisk is the direct image transfer method. Place a square of frisk over the flying saucer drawing, smooth it down, and then gently burnish along the lines. If you do not have a burnisher any hard, round-ended object should do just as well. When you lift up the frisk you will find that the outline of the flying saucer has been transferred straight onto it.

5 Cover the print with a sheet of detail paper, leaving a 'window' cut out of it where the flying saucer is to go. Next, place your piece of frisk down over this window, again rubbing over to make sure that there is no air trapped underneath it. As you can see here, the 'window' in the paper is cut smaller than the square of frisk to prevent any accidental spray onto the rest of the print.

6 You can now carefully cut out and remove the frisk from the first area to be sprayed — the underside of the flying saucer. Take care not to apply too much pressure when cutting, as you do not want to gouge great lines in the print. Spray this area with a watercolour mix of Payne's grey and white.

3

4

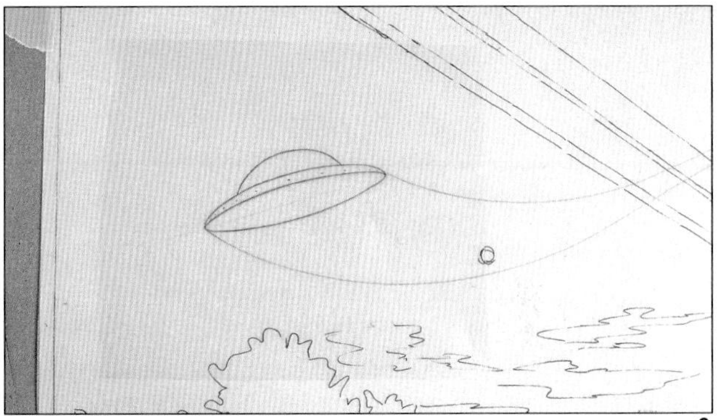

5

6

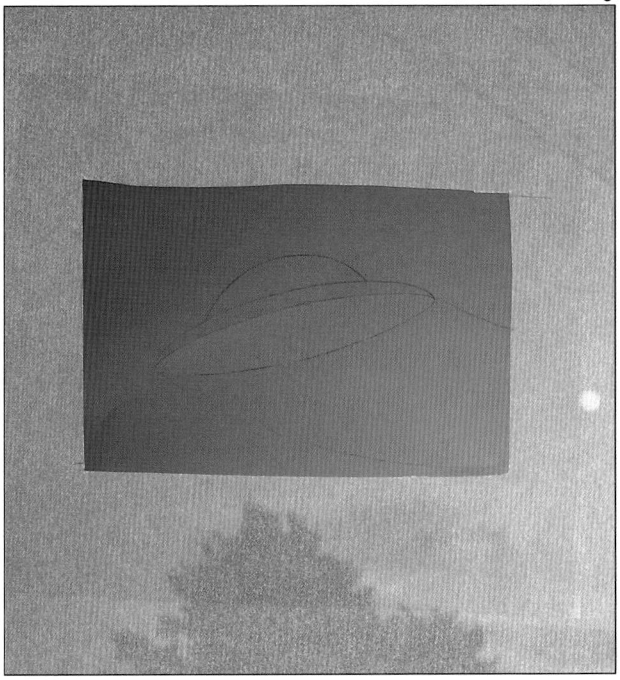

7

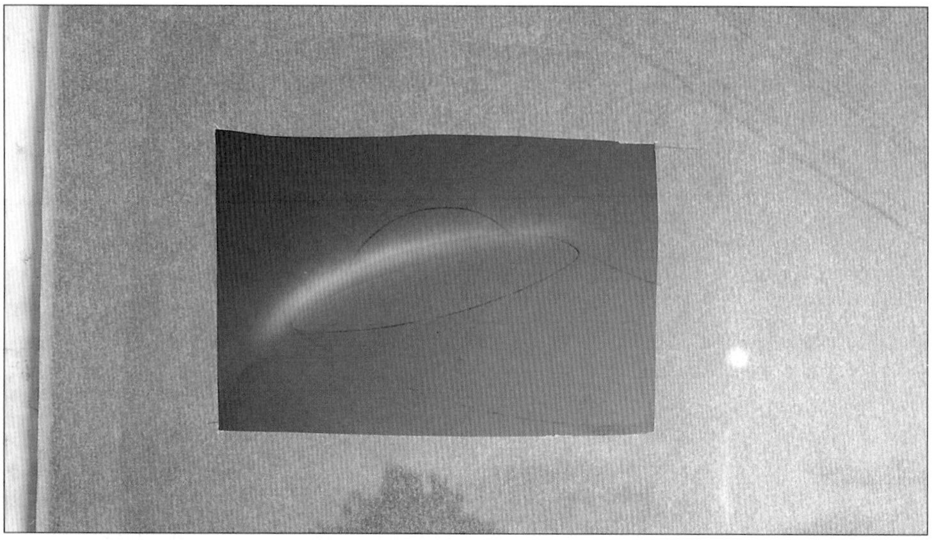

8

9

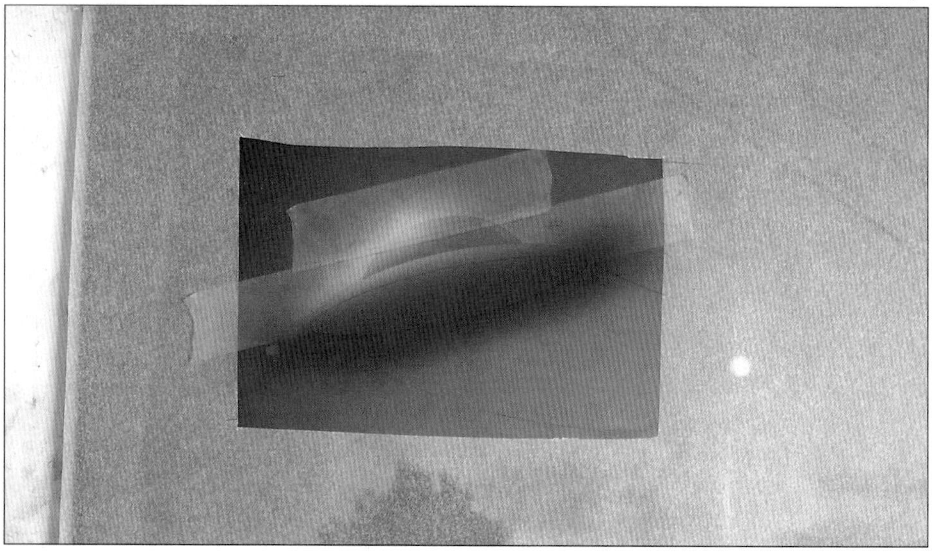

7 Test the sharpness of your blade on a scrap of paper and cut the frisk covering the centre band of the flying saucer. Cover this area with a spray of Payne's grey and white, though this time with a much higher percentage of white. Try to gradate this area slightly so that the top is lighter, especially towards the left.

8 The final part of the flying saucer can now be cut and exposed. Spray this area with the same mix that was used on the centre section, gradating up towards the top left. Because you are working in colours which slightly mimic the sky, there is no need to cover this part entirely. You can see that the background colour does, in fact, show through, but the shape of a flying saucer is what your eyes choose to see.

9 Once all the paint is dry, cover the top with 'low tack' transparent tape, so that you can reinforce the tone on the underside without spoiling the top. As this flying saucer has such a curved shape, lay straight strips of tape — which will also cover the bottom — and then cut it with a very sharp blade to expose the underside. Using a much darker mix of Payne's grey, spray this area, gradating fractionally darker towards the bottom.

10 Remove the remainder of the frisk and the paper mask. Place the paper mask on an old sheet of card, and extend the window in it so that you can now get on with the 'whoosh' lines. You can then tape this back down over the print. With a fresh rectangle of frisk — larger than your new window — transfer the 'whoosh' lines onto it from your drawing, again using the direct image transfer method, and place this on top of the print.

11 Carefully cut and expose this entire area, making sure that the flying saucer is covered with frisk. Spray over with a gentle wash of white, more towards the saucer and slowly petering out along the trail. Do not lay too much white, instead keep it just as a suggestion of colour for a really good 'whoosh'. Finally, remove all the masks to see your own photographic evidence that flying saucers really do exist.

10

11

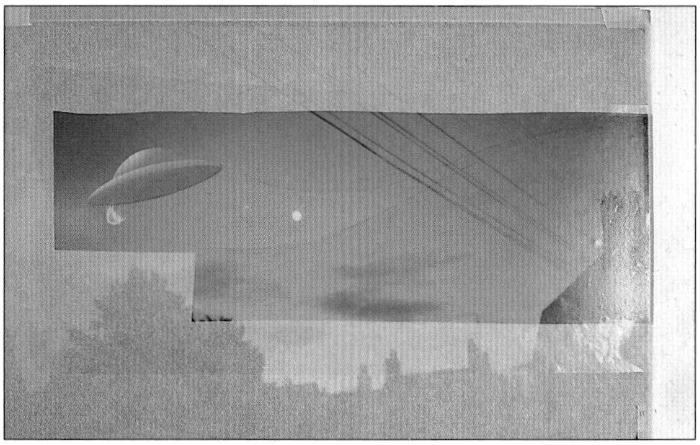

Chapter 7

Pattern making

Pattern making is really enjoyable and proves how interesting effects can be achieved through one simple image. You do not even have any freehand drawing to worry about, since these basic shapes are all around you if you keep your eyes open.

Of course, books are always an invaluable source of reference material, but everyday items can also be used. To prove this point we used a spade sign from a pack of cards, a musical note on an old sheet of music, and the fleur-de-lys came from a carrier bag. Remember, it is possible to blow anything up on a photocopier or scale up using the grid method.

The beauty of pattern making is that it is so easy to apply to almost any surface. Create your own for a frieze around the room, on a lampshade, or just to 'frame' your artwork. Whatever your preference, there is endless scope for fun so do not restrict your ambitions.

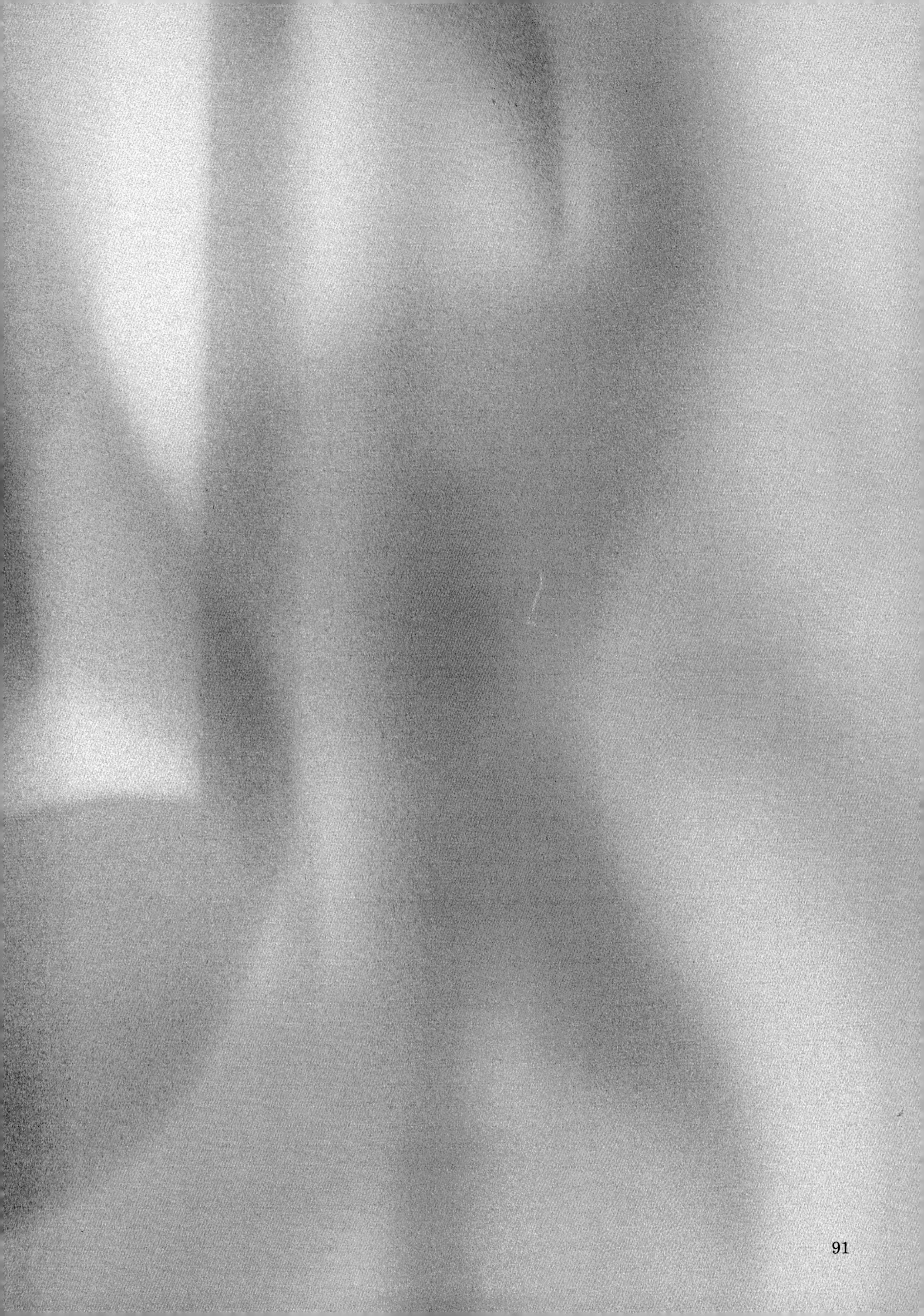

Pattern making

SPADE

Although a spade and a musical note might appear to be two of the most basic, and therefore rather dull shapes, it is for this very reason that they were chosen. The main objective of this exercise is to show you once and for all, that even while concentrating and practising on perfecting your technique with the airbrush, without wasting any time on your drawing skills, some truly amazing results can be achieved.

1 Prepare your support and then mark out and cut your choice of pattern in a piece of hard card, and hold this flat over the support. As your aim is to create an interesting result by overlapping one shape, there is no need to spray in the whole area.

2 By spraying round the outside edges of the shape, when you remove the card mask you are left with a beautifully crisp outline.

1

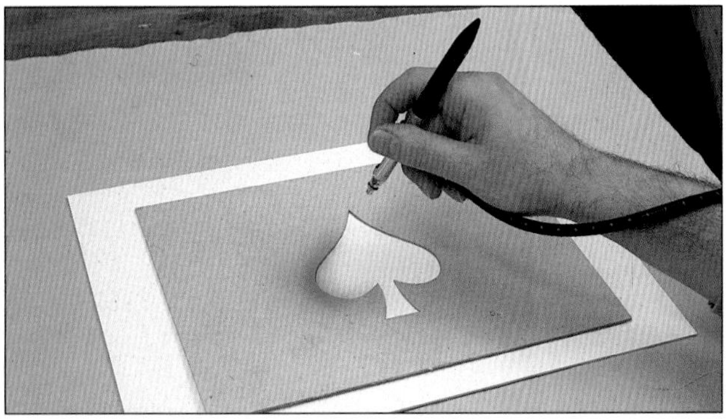

2

3

3 Re-place your mask slightly to the left of your first image. It is essential that you pick a point of reference on the initial shape so that you can repeat it as many times as you want with the spacing between each image always the same. You can see that in this example the stalk of the second spade is right in the middle of the lowest part of the left-hand side of the first.

4 Again spray round the edge of your mask to give a crisp outline and to add some body to the image.

4

5 Move your mask over to the right, and carefully re-place it using your reference point. It could also be a help to draw a line where the top of your mask sits on the support so that you do not move up or down.

5

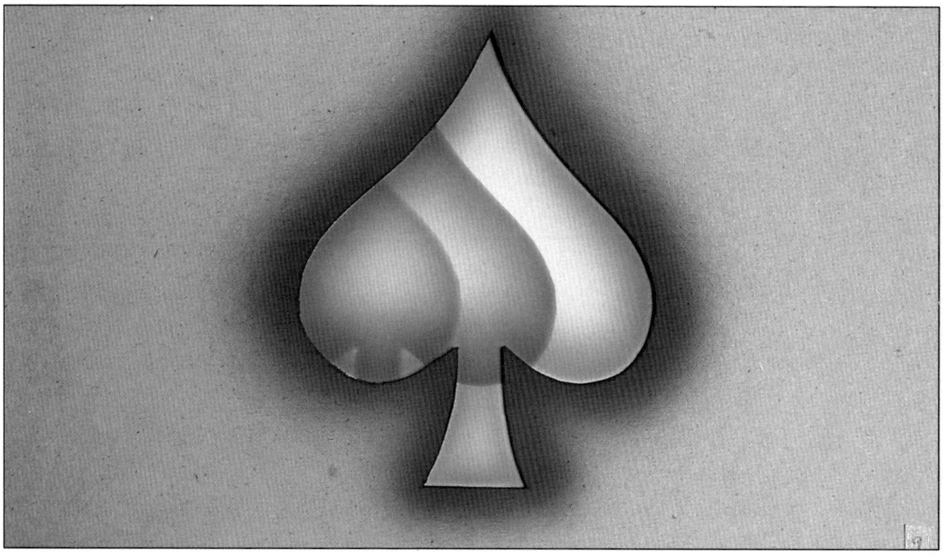

6 This process of spraying and moving your mask can be repeated as many times as you wish.

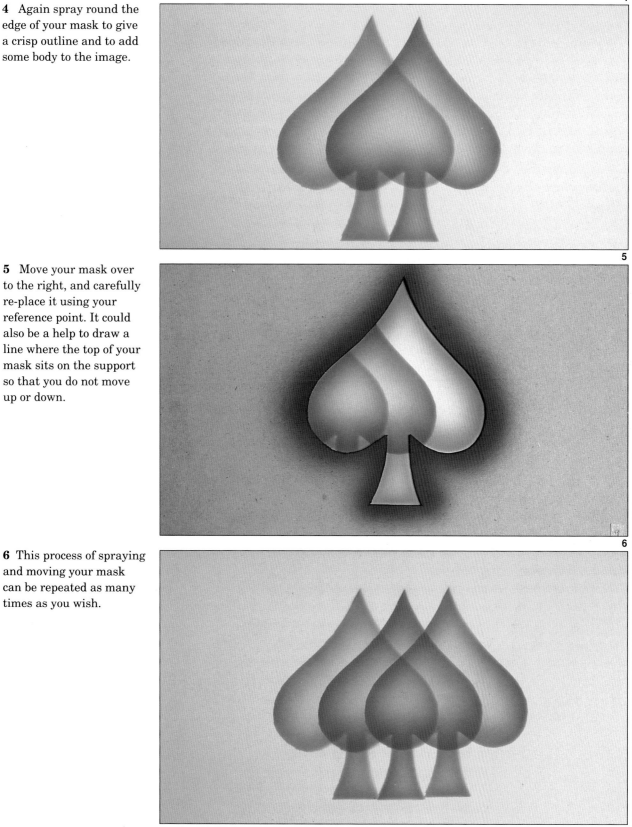

6

1a

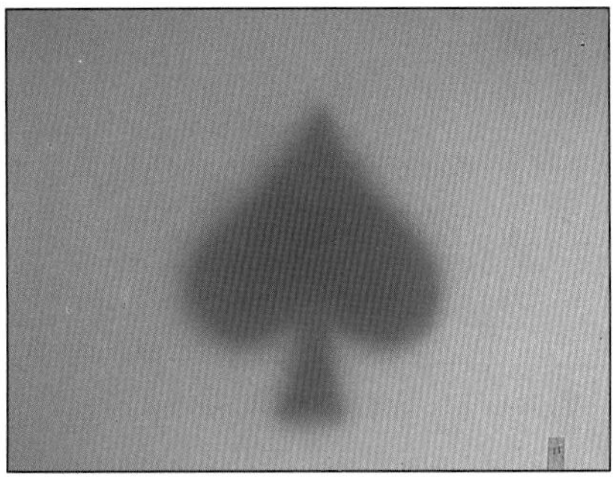

1b

1a & 1b In the previous exercise you can see the hard outline obtained by laying your mask on the support. However, equally interesting results can be achieved with the mask held above it. If you lift your mask up slightly and spray a flat colour over it you will get an almost misty image.

2a

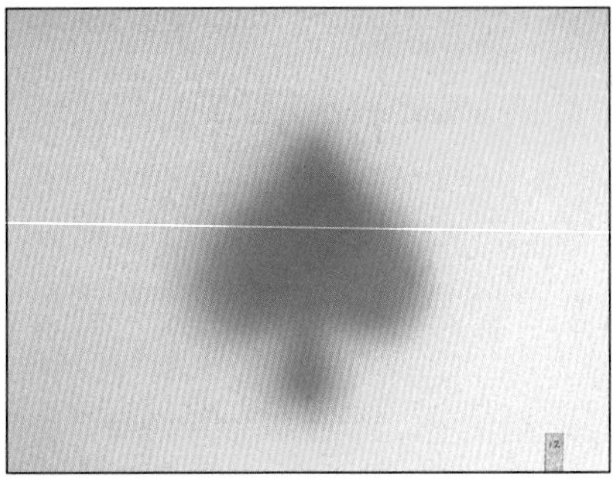

2b

2a & 2b If the mask is held further away still, not only will the image become very blurred and dream-like, but the spray itself will be very diffused and have a lovely texture.

1

1 Repeated, overlapping patterns need not be regimented and orderly. You can be abstract and colourful and still produce a beautiful effect. Cut a stylised musical note from a piece of hard board, place it on your support and gently spray over it

2

2 Move your mask and spray over it again, but with a different colour. Remember always to flush your airbrush through between colours.

3

4

3 Continue moving your mask and spraying different colours - some with the mask on the support and some with it held at different heights. By doing this you will not only get a contrast of colour but also a variety of strength of image, (see picture 4).

FLEURS DE LYS

It is hoped that throughout your own experimentations with overlapping patterns, you have managed to succeed in creating some weird and wonderful designs. Now you can see that by using a simple outline shape in a more regimented fashion, equally bold patterns can be formed. Just imagine how effective this fleur-de-lys would look sprayed in gold onto a plain window pelmet or cupboard doors. The combinations are endless, and allow you to make your own individual stamp, even in your own home.

1 Do your initial drawing of a fleur-de-lys on a piece of paper. With a shape such as this it is vital that both sides match, so a ruled line down the centre is of enormous help if you are drawing it freehand. It may be a good idea to cheat and just to trace the image here, but take extra care when you scale it up.

2 Cover your drawing with acetate, and with a sharp scalpel cut out the outline of the fleur-de-lys using your drawing as a guide.

1

2

3 Put the acetate on your support, stretch it out and take the corners. Acetate, unlike frisk, does not stick down, so to stop any of it lifting in the centre place a few coins around the cut-out stencil.

4 Cover with a spray of sky blue, gradating it from top to bottom to add interest. You can see here the outlines of the coins which were used to hold the acetate down.

3

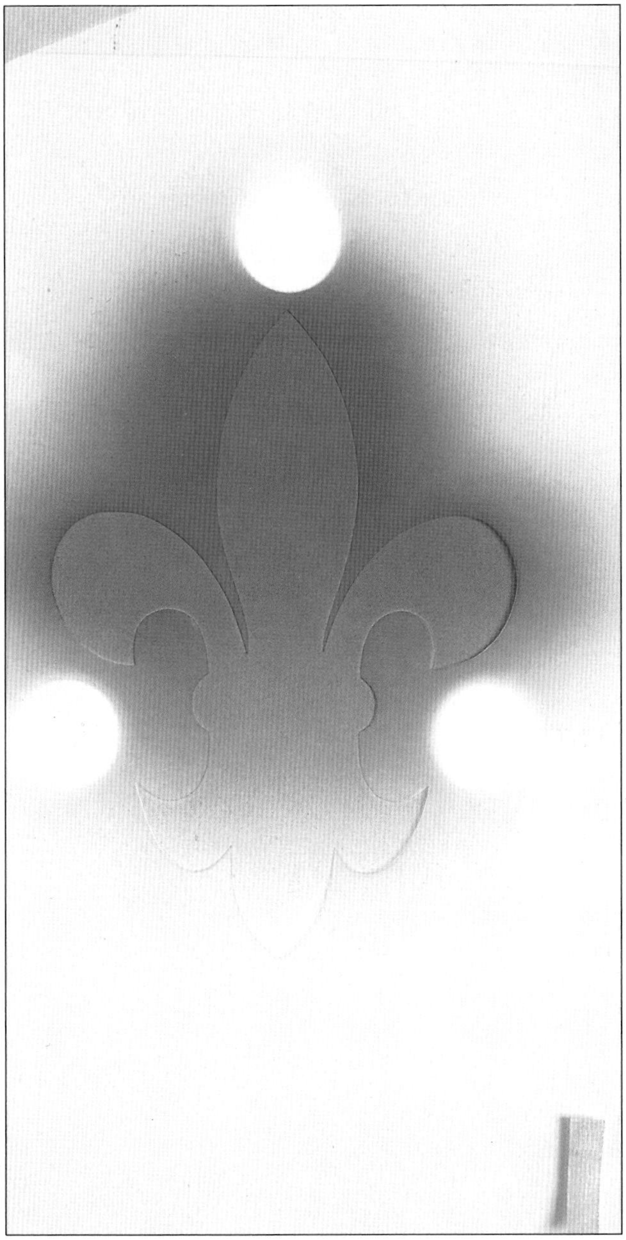

4

5 Lift off the acetate and place it carefully to one side. The result at this stage can be closely checked to make sure you are happy with your stencil before you continue. You will note that where the coins were placed the stencil has produced a very hard outline, and further away from these points the outline is very slightly blurred. This, together with the gradation of colour, helps to give the image a lovely sense of 'falling away' towards the bottom and accentuates the three points of the fleur-de-lys.

6 Re-place the stencil onto the support to one side of your first image. Since acetate is transparent, it is very easy to lay it wherever you fancy by eye. You again need to tape the corners of the acetate and place a few coins on top of it. Spray over with the same gradation from top to bottom as before.

5

6

7

7 You can continue to move your stencil and spray further fleur-de-lys shapes to create as long a pattern as you wish. The result is an attractive frieze which was incredibly easy to make.

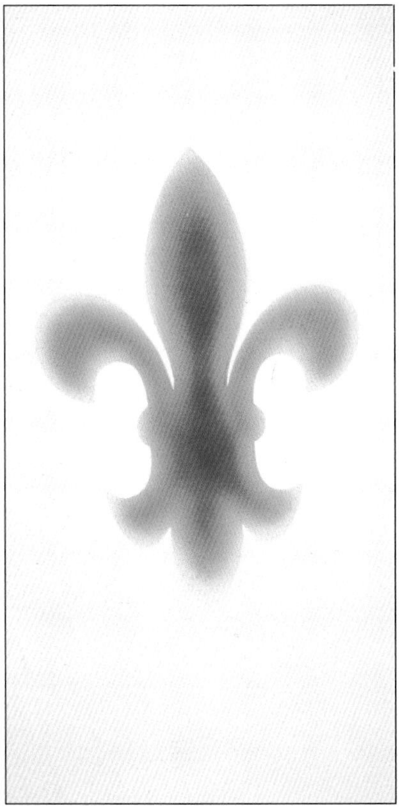

Although a gradation of colour from top to bottom is a wonderful effect, with a stencil such as this there are no hard and fast rules as to how it should be sprayed. Here are some suggestions for alternative ways to spray it, but in fact the only real limitation to what you can do is the extent of your imagination.

yellow fleur-de-lys
Here a dense yellow was sprayed close to the support and around the outline of the fleur-de-lys only.

red fleur-de-lys
In this case red was sprayed from a slight height and in a rough circle following the general shape of the fleur-de-lys.

green fleur-de-lys
Green has been sprayed quite close to the support, following the outline, but spraying away from the edges and towards the centre.

blue outline
Finally, instead of using the normal acetate stencil, here the part that was cut out has been used and blue sprayed round its outline — so giving a white image on a blue background.

Chapter 8

Lettering

The aim of most of the projects in this book is to show you how interesting and professional-looking results can be accomplished, without having to be a Michelangelo. Simple lettering is no exception. With a good old pencil and a sheet of tracing paper anything is possible.

By far your most useful reference in this area will be a catalogue of typefaces. The most easily obtainable are the catalogues that are produced by the manufacturers of dry transfer lettering. These are cheap and readily available from any art suppliers. The range is limitless, and if you are feeling particularly creative you can combine two or more together for some really original and wacky effects.

Once again inspiration can be found anywhere — some unusual lettering rendered by the airbrush artist Phil Dobson, was based on the floor indicator of an Art-Deco hotel lift. So do keep your eyes peeled.

Lettering

CIRCUS LETTERING

In the following project the aim is to show you how even by 'cheating' and using a typeface taken directly from a catalogue, you can achieve an original piece of lettering. So if you are not feeling creative, or simply do not have the time, your own originality can be added to a traced typeface by your choice of colours. The very word 'Circus' immediately conjures up images of fun and colour. So instead of just copying what has been done here, create your own colour combinations. You will be amazed as to how individual and different it will look.

1

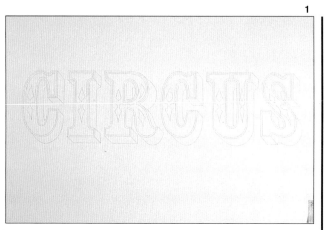

2

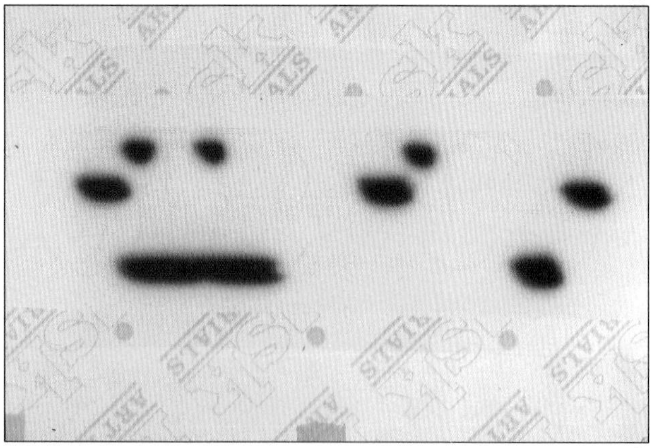

3

1 First work out your lettering as a line drawing on gridded paper to enable you to make sure the proportions are correct and that you are totally happy with it. Then transfer it onto your chosen support with transtrace paper so that you have a clean line drawing from which you can make a proper start.

2 Completely cover the line drawing with frisk and with a sharp blade carefully cut your first mask. This is for the darkest shadowed areas of the lettering because you want to start with the darkest areas first and work up to the lightest. Once you have them exposed, spray over with a red ochre gouache.

3 Do not remove the frisk, but now cut out the next darkest areas of the letter shadows. Again spray over with red ochre, this time, though, use the edge of a piece of paper as a movable mask to give your shadows some linear edges.

4

4 You can now expose the lightest parts of the shadows, and once more spray over with red ochre. The first sections you exposed will now have been sprayed three times and so the shadowed areas will show a gradation of light to dark

5

5 Remove the original frisk and you will see that your lettering has a nice solid look to it thanks to the shadowing. Lay down a fresh sheet of frisk, and then very carefully cut all the remaining lines into it.

6 The trick here is to spray two shades of the same colour, scarlet, separately which will produce a third shade where they overlap, and thus give your lettering much more depth. Expose the area for your first shade of colour and spray over.

6

7

8

7 Next, remove the frisk from your second area of shade and again spray over. Continue to use scarlet as your colour but only spray it at about half the strength as you did for the first area of shade. You will see that where the second mask only was sprayed — the very outline of the lettering — you will have a very pale scarlet, and the area on the face of the lettering where you have sprayed twice will be a much darker shade.

8 Expose the final area of lettering and then spray over the whole lot with a transparent yellow. This will give you a solid yellow for the bottom half of the lettering and turn the scarlet at the top slightly orange. Do not be tempted to remove the frisk yet.

9

9 Although your lettering will now look complete, it can be further enhanced by adding a sheen. This is very simple and will add a very professional, finished look. Using a loose paper mask for linear edges spray over very lightly with an opaque white, and as a final touch add a gradation of white across the bottom of the letters. Finally remove and discard your frisk mask.

10

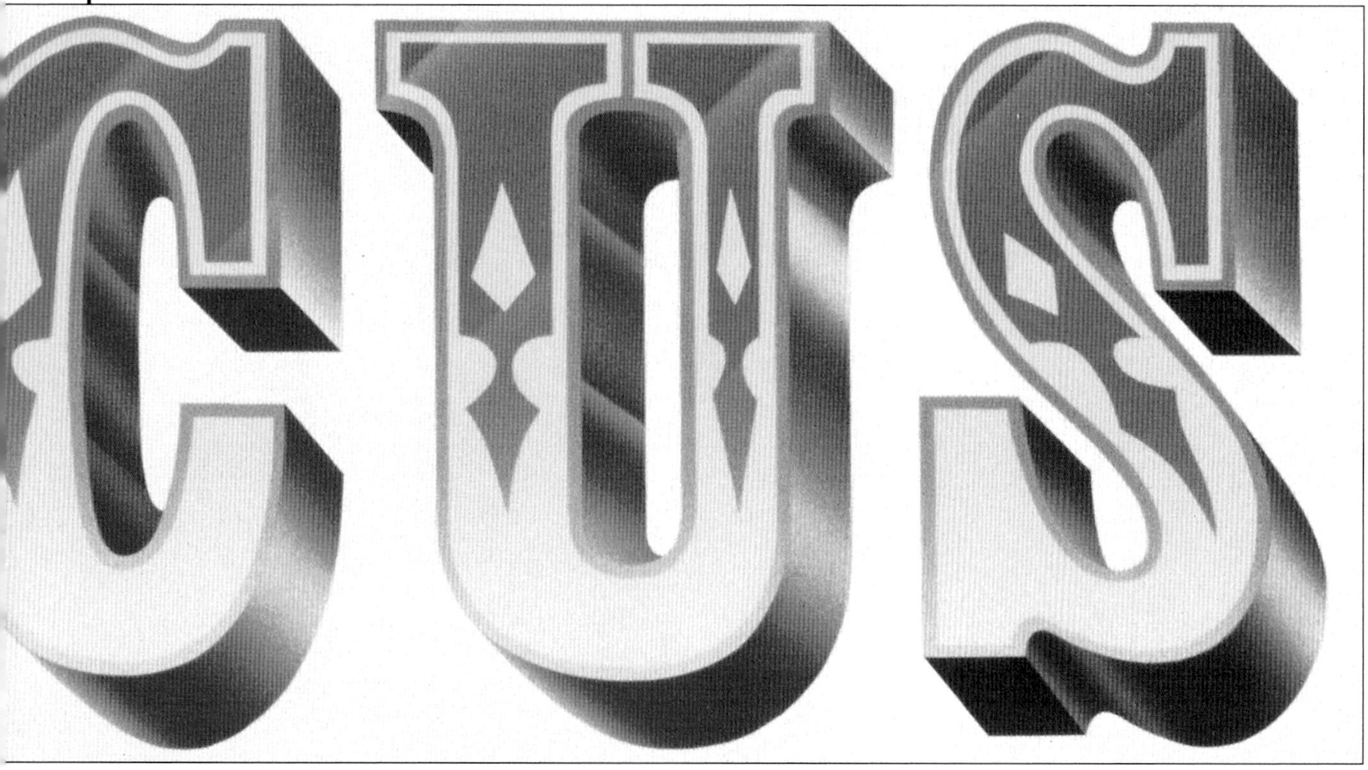

DECO LETTERING

Since the previous lettering exercise was to encourage you by keeping things simple, this following project is a little more taxing. Although this technique is the same as employed on the last project, it is used in a far more complex and therefore time-consuming way. However, you must have already built up your level of patience just by reaching this point of the book, and the stunning end results that can be reached through the use of a chrome effect in lettering will certainly prove well worth the effort. Although a little improvisation was used in the construction of this lettering, it was all based on easily accessible reference material.

1

2

3

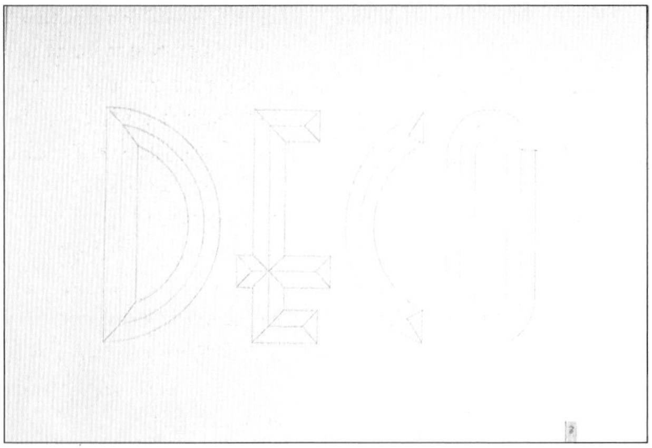

4

1 Draw up your lettering on detail paper, making sure that you show all the different angles of the three-dimensional effect. The style of the lettering here was partly sourced from magazines, with a fair deal just made up — there are no hard and fast rules as to what you can and cannot do with lettering.

2 Transfer the initial drawing to your support using transtrace. Take your time to make sure that all the curves in particular are perfect. Your masks will be cut from this drawing so it is very important that you get it right.

3 Remove the sheet of transtrace, and before you go any further clean your support with a small amount of lighter fuel. The transtrace tends to leave some 'sootiness' on the support, and this could become a problem when you lay your frisk since it will not adhere to the support as well as it should.

4 Now cover your support with a layer of frisk, smoothing it out to make sure that there are no creases or bumps in it. Do not throw away the backing to the frisk since this will come in very handy latter on. Using a very sharp blade — preferably a brand new one — cut the frisk along the lines of your drawing.

5

6

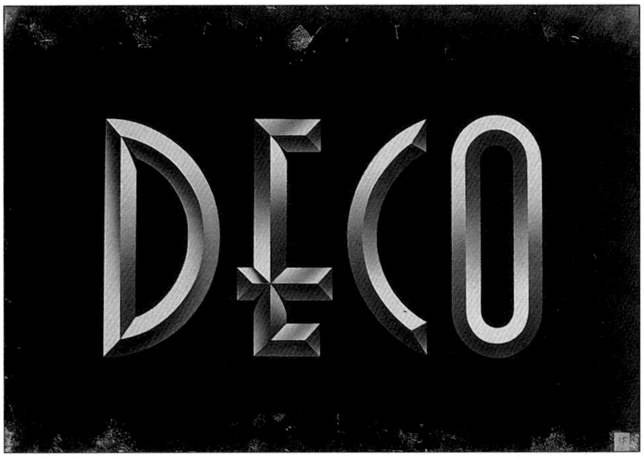

5 Carefully peel off the frisk covering the background, making sure that all the letters remain totally covered. Spray over the whole background with a solid black. Since your lettering is going to have a metal effect, a black background will greatly enhance its impact.

6 Remove the tiny masks covering the darkest parts of the lettering and spray over these with a mix of lamp black with a few drops of ultramarine. This mixture creates a Payne's grey which is perfect for chrome: you can buy Payne's grey from various manufacturers but these can vary so much in colour that it is much safer to mix your own. Since these are sprayed very dark there is no need to replace the masks.

7 Peel back the mask covering the outside upright of the 'D', but do not remove it completely, instead hold it out of the way with a piece of tape. Spray this area with your 'own brand' Payne's grey, gradating the colour from dark at the top to almost nonexistent at the bottom. Since you are trying to achieve a polished metal effect you do not want to allow this area to be over-sprayed as you continue, so once the paint is dry re-cover it with its mask.

7

8

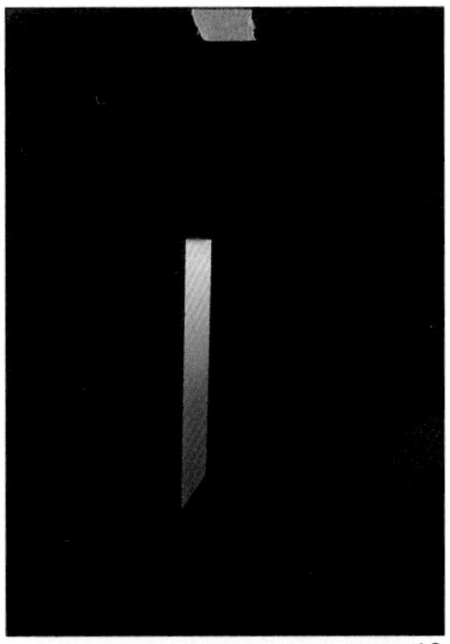

9

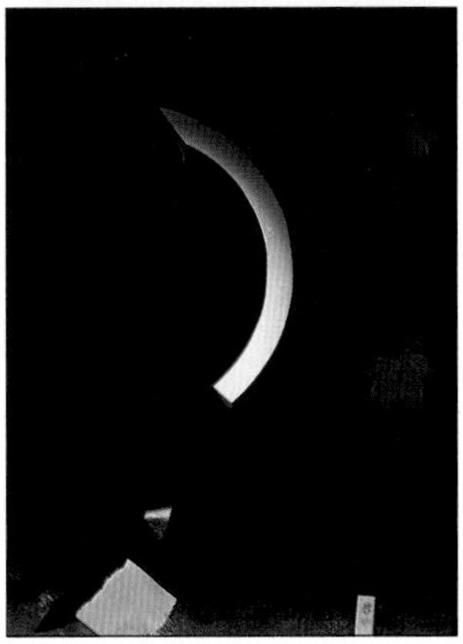

10

8 The inside curve of the 'D' is now exposed. Using your same colour mix spray a gradation of tone from top to bottom, allowing the board to show through quite clearly.

9 This same process can now be repeated for the inside upright, this time gradating from bottom to top. Make sure that when you hinge the mask out of the way with tape, that you do not stick the tape onto the background — which when removed could lift up the black — it should be on the outside border of frisk.

10 Finally the outside curve can be removed and sprayed with a gradation of tone from bottom to top. By reversing the gradation on the inside to the outside of the 'D' you will have created a contrast which will give this letter its three-dimensional effect.

11

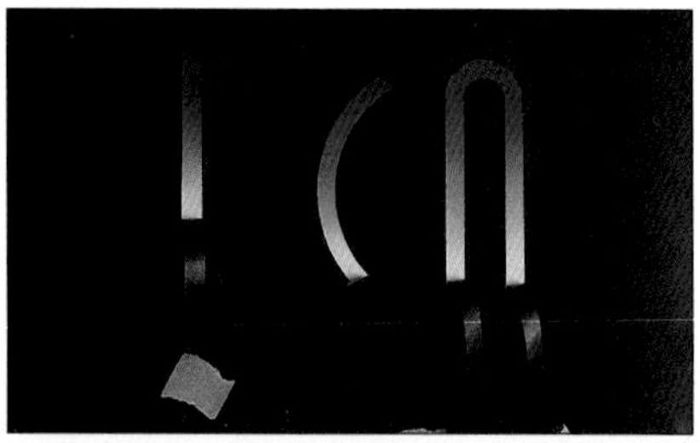

12

13

14

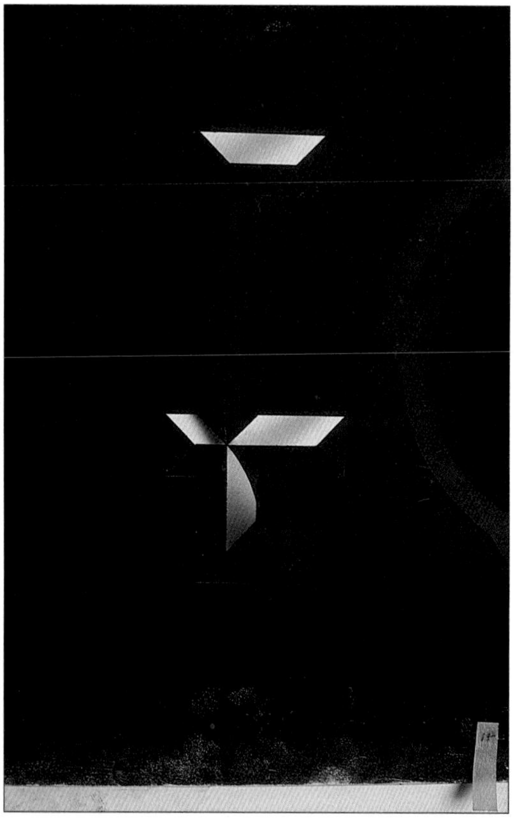

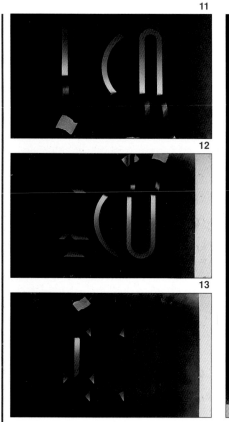

11, 12, 13, 14 Now repeat this process of peeling back masks and spraying gradated tones for the remainder of the letters. You can either spray one letter at a time or, as was done here, throw caution to the wind and do all similar areas at once. Where your masks are too small to be hinged out of the way (on the 'E' and the end of the 'C') remove them completely, put them onto your saved piece of frisk backing paper, and carefully replace them once you have sprayed the areas. Do not rush this process by removing too many masks at once, and make sure that the inside and outside edges of your letters have opposite gradation.

15

15 It is now safe to completely remove all the masks covering the letters. You can see that due to the gradating of colour within each area of your lettering, they are now starting to take on the look of chrome.

16

17

16 & 17 If you do a close inspection of your lettering you may well find that some paint has bled under the edges of the frisk. This is, in fact, what has happened to the upright of the 'D' in the example shown here. Do not panic since this is easy to put right by very gently scratching it off with a sharp scalpel blade.

18

18 To further enhance your lettering you can now add some linear detail too the highlighted areas by scratching back with a curved scalpel blade, and rubbing back with an eraser for a softer edge. Use the frisk backing paper to rest your hand on while you are doing this, or you could easily spoil your artwork. You also need to add a highlight to the high-point line of the letters, again by scratching back with your curved scalpel blade.

19 As a finishing touch you can now add a flare to the strongest areas of highlight. This is done by spraying a roughly circular patch freehand with opaque white. Keep these gentle and do not lay down too much white which could totally ruin the effect.

19

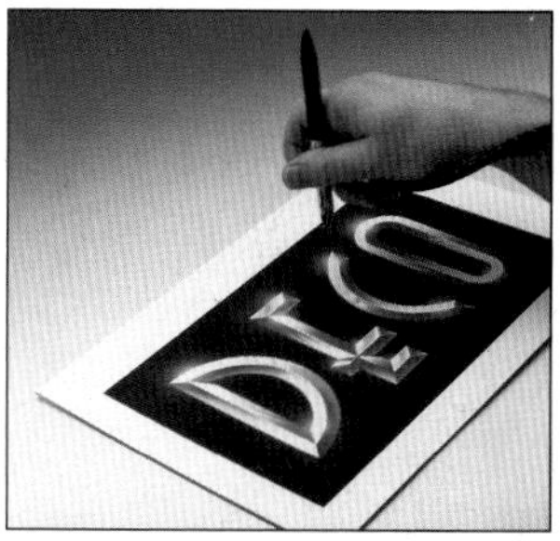

Chapter 9

Contrasting media

It is without question that the original type of medium which was used in conjunction with the airbrush was of a transparent quality. Even Charles Burdick, who is credited with the invention of the tool, was a watercolourist himself, and of course through its development as a photo-retouching tool, a transparent medium was the simple and obvious choice. The techniques involved in airbrushing, especially over-spraying, readily lend themselves to a transparent medium.

Soon, however, artists ventured to test out other types of media. No doubt several airbrushes were relegated to the scrap heap due to irreparable clogging, but problems such as these have to be swallowed when playing the role of an innovator. Through the process of trial and error it was discovered that equally stunning results could be achieved with an opaque medium, and although some advantages were lost, others were gained.

The aim of the following projects is not just to show you the contrast between transparent and opaque media, but also to introduce you to the fact that 'real art' is possible with an airbrush.

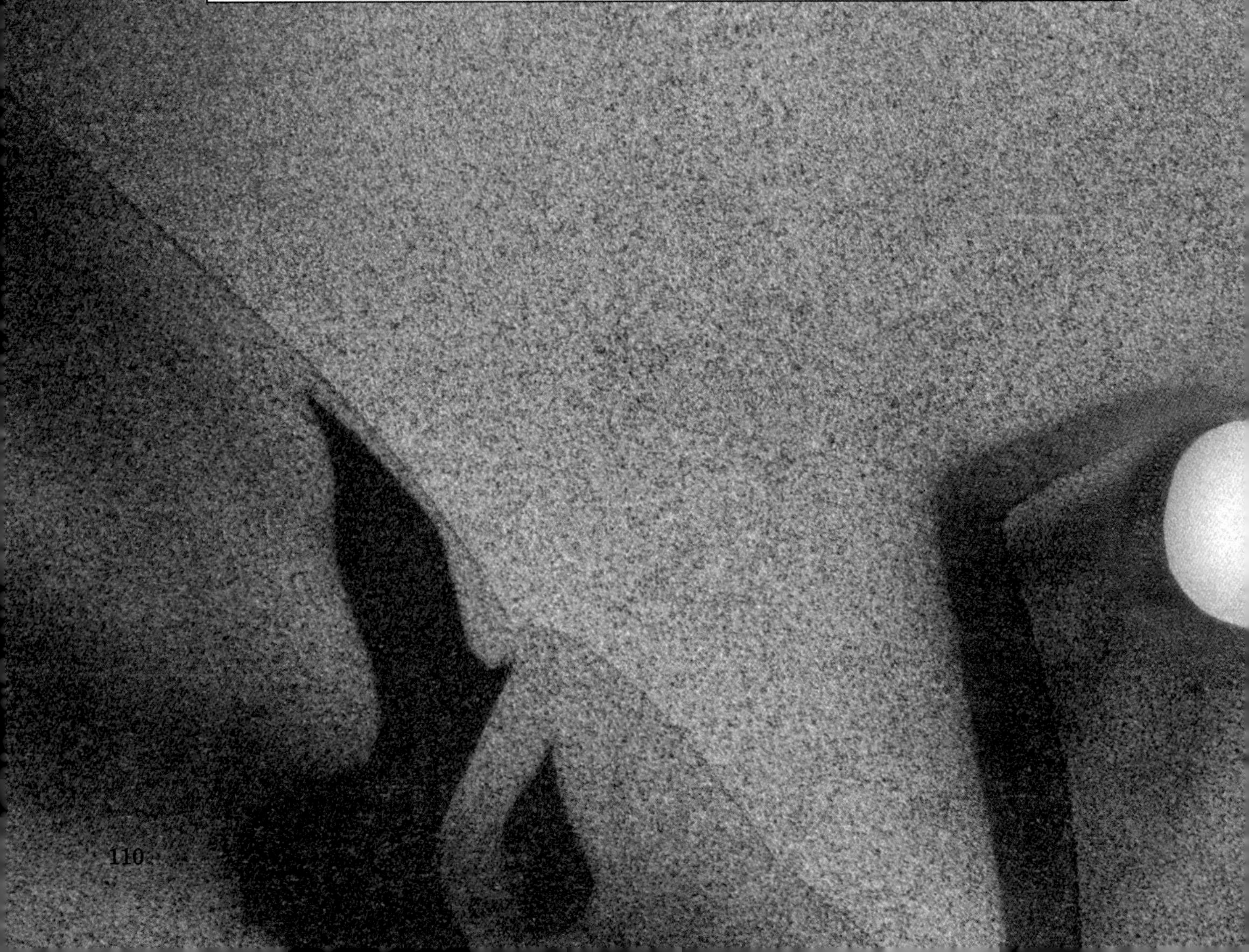

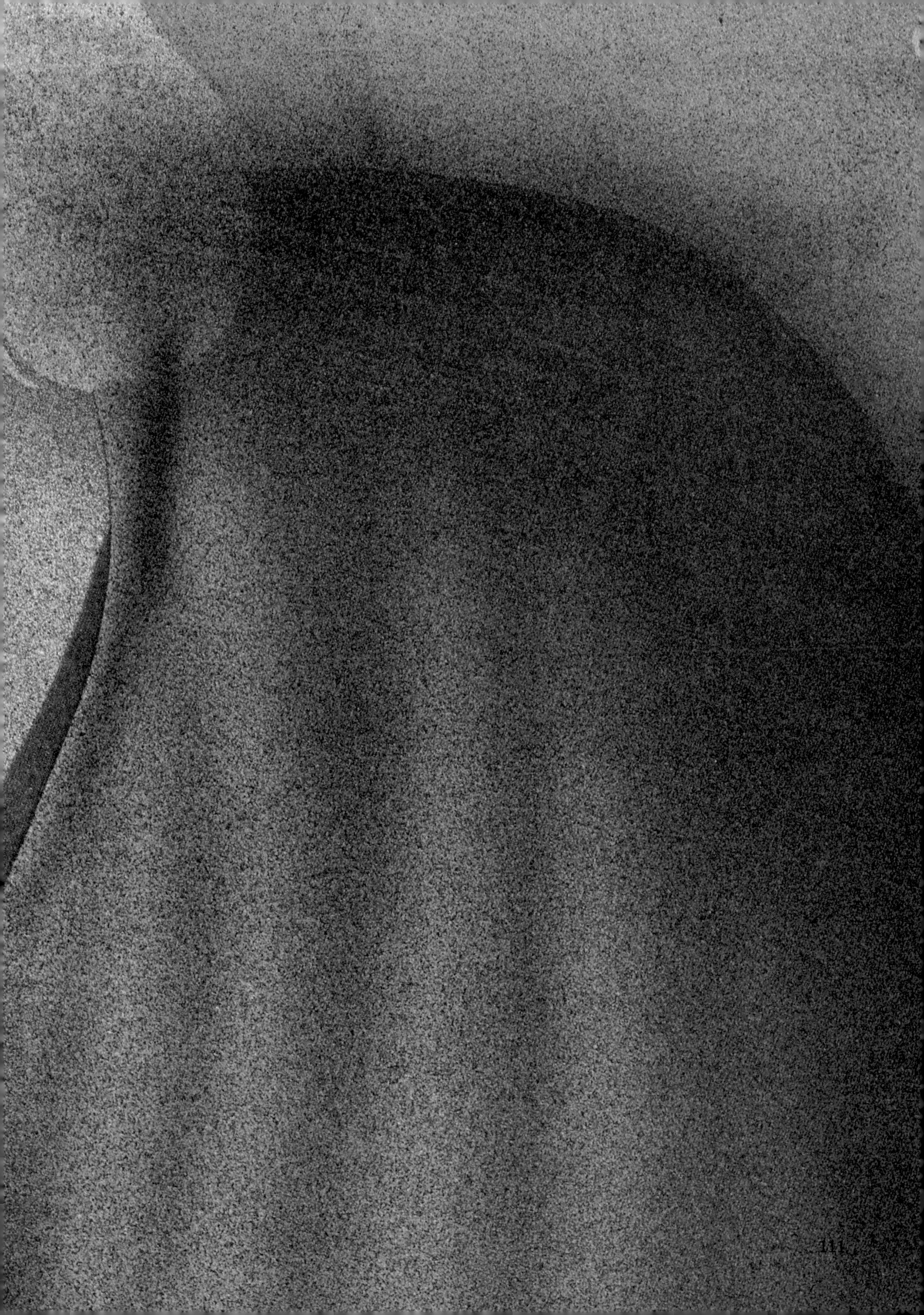

Contrasting media

TRANSPARENT IMAGE

While you have been working your way through this book you will have realised that transparent media are the most favoured. The advantages of working from dark to light should already be apparent — any over-spray occurring with this method will only enhance your darker shading, not obliterate it. This also allows you more control as you can build up your tones gradually as you go. On the other hand, there are restrictions; mistakes are much more difficult to correct as it is impossible to cover over an error. So far you have been made aware of the enormous range of effects that can be achieved when working with this medium. It is hoped that you will also have had some fun, so it is about time to produce an image that will prove a real challenge.

1

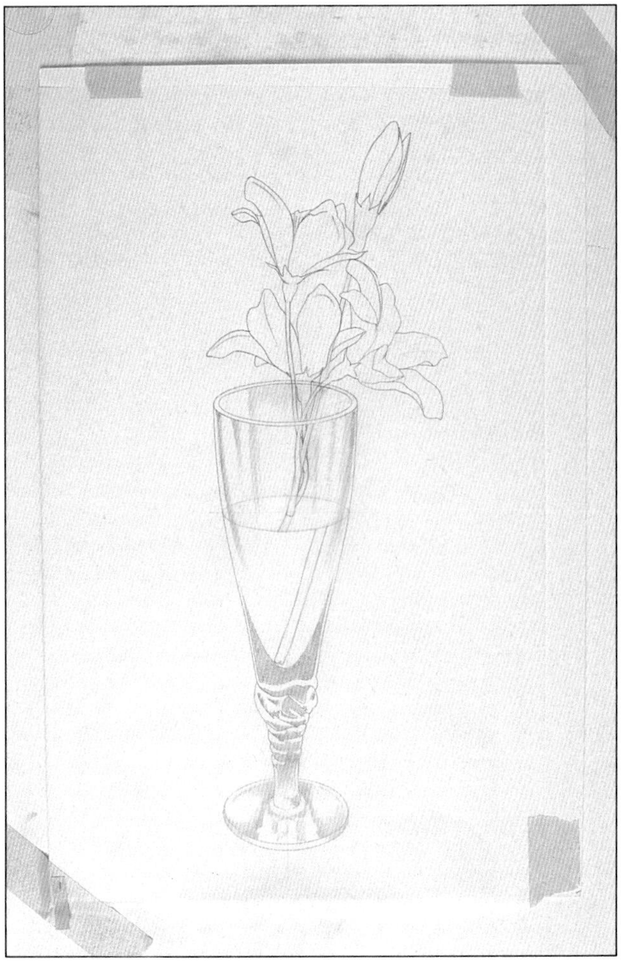

2

1 Rough out your initial sketch on a piece of detail paper, making sure that you show the areas of light and dark for reference later on. Make any alterationsat this stage, as they will be harder to change once you have started. Transfer the drawing to your support using transtrace, taking care as you go. Any pencil marks will be reproduced on the board. Do not transfer the shading, as this will show through the watercolours. Remove the transtrace, and wipe over with lighter fuel.

2 You can now cover the support with a layer of frisk, making sure that there are no air bubbles lurking under it, and cut along the outline of the glass and the flowers so that the background can be exposed. Peel back the frisk covering the background — hinging it with some tape so that it can be easily replaced once the paint is dry — and spray a gradated tone of Payne's grey over the area from top to bottom.

3

3 Do not replace the background mask just yet, but rather spray an extremely light coat of Hooker's green over the complete area. This does not need to be gradated like the Payne's grey, since, as long as you keep it light, the gradation beneath it will still be very noticeable.

4

4 The last detail for the background can now be added. Using an equal mix of Payne's grey and Hooker's green, spray a freehand gradated shadow to the glass. If you feel nervous about potentially ruining your artwork, start very lightly and slowly build up this shadow, as you will then be able to stop at the precise moment you are happy with your result.

5

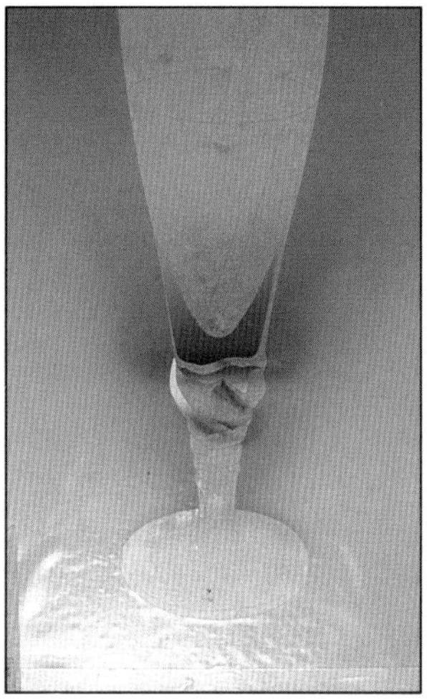

5 Once everything is dry, fold the background mask back into place. Just to make sure there are no small exposed areas around the flowers, use some 'low tack' tape to completely cover this part of your work. Your first masks on the glass itself can now be removed and sprayed with Payne's grey. These are the very darkest areas at the base of the glass.

6

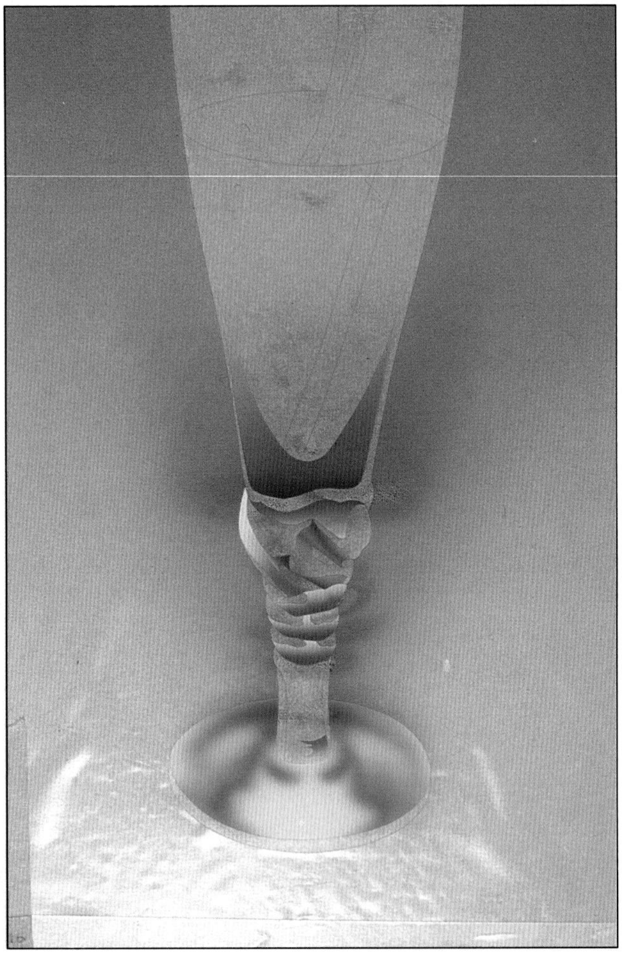

7

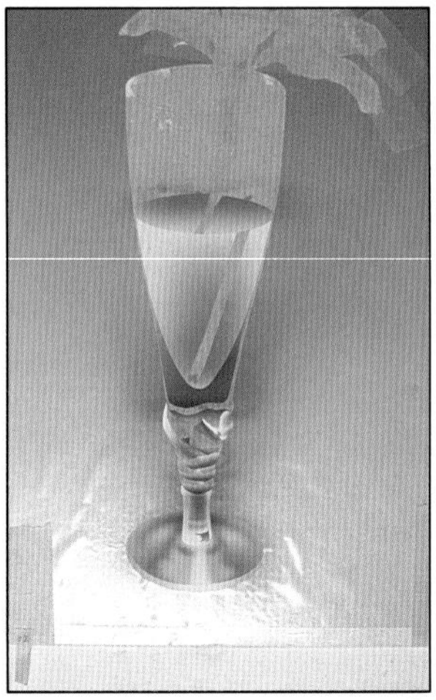

8

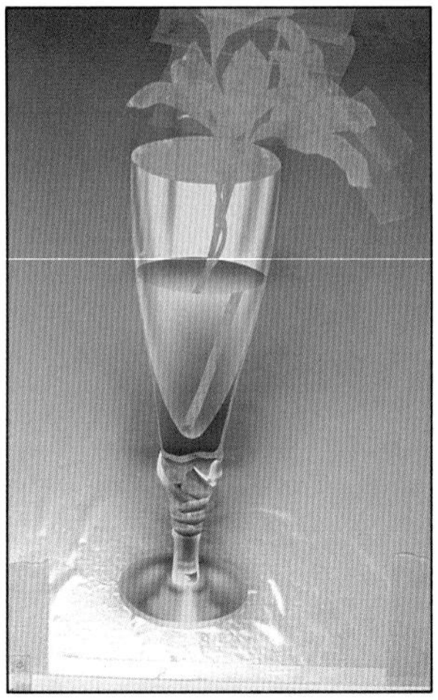

9

6 As you are working in watercolours it is most important that you always work from dark to light, since not only can you increase the intensity of shade by spraying further washes on top of existing ones, but also because any accidental overspray of lighter tones will not show up. So, working from dark to light, gradually remove the masks and continue to spray the exposed areas with Payne's grey, progressing slowly down the stem and onto the base of the glass. The base will provide you with the prefect opportunity to practise your freehand control as you try to create the gentle curves within it. Do not worry if your attempt is not quite up to the level shown here, as the artist in this case has had years of practice.

7 The remaining masks for Payne's grey on the glass stem can now be removed and sprayed with light washes, adding some freehand detail of tone where you feel it is necessary. Next, the edge of the base, the top of the water and the front side of water can be removed in turn, and sprayed with gradated tones. Do not try to spray inside the masks, but instead make sweeps right across them.

8 The frisk covering the remainder of the front of the glass can now be carefully peeled off. Spray this area very lightly all over with your Payne's grey. The glass will be unnaturally light, but don't be tempted into laying too dark a colour as you will be over-spraying it. Before continuing, add some darker curved lines down the front by spraying freehand.

9 Remove the mask covering the top of the glass, and spray the whole of the body. To achieve the best results it may be a help to turn your artwork on its side so that you can spray from the top to the bottom of the glass in more natural left, right sweeps. Try to gradate the colour so that you get lighter bands running down the glass. You will see that, because you lightly sprayed the front of the glass first and then over-sprayed it, the glass now has a lovely sense of depth to it. Once everything is dry you can remove the frisk covering the lip of the glass and very gently lay a wash over it.

10 The frisk covering the side outlines of the glass and the final parts of the stem can now be peeled off with a scalpel. Very gently spray these areas with Hooker's green so that just a tint is added, and then spray a soft tone, again in Hooker's green, right down the centre of the glass. This will create the illusion of the glass picking up the background colour and so greatly add to the realism of your finished artwork.

10

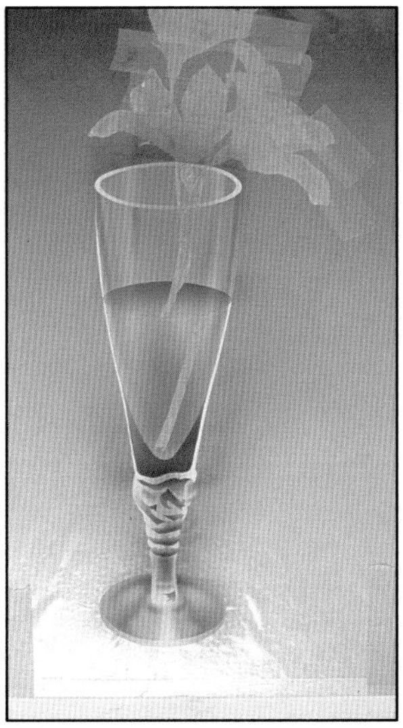

12

11

11 You can now remove all the 'low tack' tape and remaining masking, even though you are only half-way through. This is because you will have totally unmasked the glass by now, and to replace all the tiny bits on the stem accurately would probably take longer than spraying the entire artwork! Cover the whole image with fresh frisk and carefully cut the masking for the flowers' various stems and their shared main stem.

12 Remove the masking from the darkest areas of the stems. For this part of the project it would be a good idea to further work out the dark and light areas on your initial drawing with coloured felt-tip pens. This will give you a ready made 'colour chart' that you can keep referring back to. Spray these darkest areas in dark green.

13

15

14

13 Gradually work through the stems, systematically removing each piece of masking in turn and spraying carefully, but make sure that you leave the reflection of the main stem on the water masked since this needs to be much lighter, and will be sprayed later on. Remember also that for fine, detailed areas your airbrush should be held close to the support for maximum control.

14 Now you have completed the most intricate and difficult part of the stem, so take a deep breath and congratulate yourself. Relax, as this next step will seem like child's play. Cut and remove the mask for the refracted part of the main stem under the water and spray over in dark green, gradating it to a lighter shade nearer the water level.

15 The flowers' stems and their joint main stem are now looking very realistic, but to enhance them further some highlights must be added. Taking a fresh, curved scalpel blade gently scratch back the paint — following the shapes of the stems — to create rows of irregular lines. Obviously, you should not add these highlights to the part of the main stem under the water.

16

17

16 Finally, remove the frisk covering the main stem's reflection on the surface of the water, and spray over this area, all the small stems and the part of the main stem above water, in a light green. This is necessary because when you use the scratching back technique to add highlights the surface of your support will be showing through and can look very unnatural. Do not be lazy and try spraying this final stage with dark green to avoid a colour change as you will lose your highlight details !

17 With a sheet of fresh frisk, re-mask the whole of the artwork. Never forget that the paint you have just sprayed must always be totally dry before re-masking, because if you do not, when you come to remove all the masking for the final stage it could be disastrous with hours of hard work totally ruined.

18

19

20

21

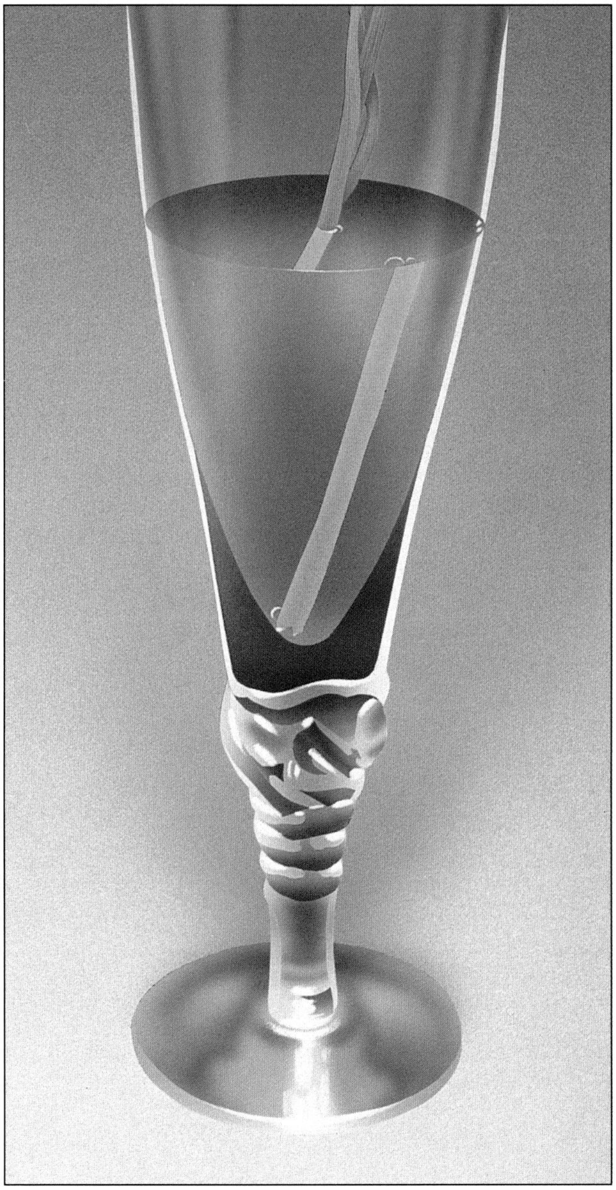

18 One cannot emphasize enough the golden rule about fresh scalpel blades. You do not need to change the blade every time you cut a new section of masking on a single artwork, but do keep checking the sharpness of your scalpel on a scrap of paper just in case. A good, clean-cut mask can easily make or break your finished piece, especially where a lot of small detail is involved. So check your blade, and if you are satisfied with it, cut into the frisk following the lines for the flowers. Remove the masking from the darkest areas of the petals and spray in scarlet lake.

19 Continue working through the petals slowly, carefully cutting and removing the masks, and always working from dark to light. When you are working on an area which is to have a natural, contoured look, make each section of masking slightly larger than you would normally for fine detail, since this will give you enough room for some freehand spraying.

20 At last you are nearing completion, and the lightest areas of the petals can now be exposed. As you can see, these last masks are the insides of the flowers. These sections will also show the contrast that is needed to differentiate between the outside and inner parts of the flowers. Spraying freehand, keep adding those little touches. Here you can see how your line control exercises have been used across the petals, and on some areas the airbrush has been held right away from the support so that when the paint hits the surface you can just see the individual spots of spray.

21 This is the last stage before you finish. With all the masking removed the final details can be added by scratching back very gently with a scalpel. Reinforce the highlights around the spiral of the glass stem, and to complete the realism, scratch back tiny circular highlights at the top and bottom of the refracted part of the main flower stem as well as where it hits the top of the water. With the addition of these tiny air bubbles the whole image comes alive.

Now that you have successfully rendered a still life, here is a complete change for you. Not only will you now be working in a different medium, but in this case you will achieve an almost photographic realism. You will soon discover opaque's good and bad points — there is no natural gradation, but you can totally cover over areas in a different colour, even light over dark. The results obtained are not necessarily unnatural, and you can see over the following pages how flesh is rendered with this medium. Please do not be put off by the finished result. After all it is all a question of confidence in yourself, and once you have read through the steps carefully, you will see the project depends on correct masking and control. However, before you attempt this project do practise the doodling exercise that was shown to you earlier on, just to get the feel of the different results produced by this medium.

1 The most useful way to start up this project is to work up your initial drawing from a live model, by getting a friend to sit for you. If this is not possible, or if you are not a skilled artist, your best form of reference is a photograph. This will also help you to work out your areas of dark and light. Also you could 'cheat' and trace, or even scale up directly from it. Whichever method you choose, your first step will always be a pencil drawing.

2 Once you are totally satisfied with your drawing, take a sheet of transtrace paper and transfer it onto your support. Remember not to throw the transtrace away as you can use it more than once. Notice how the shading has not been transferred onto the support, but just the outlines. As you are using an opaque medium the shading might not show through, but it could create an uneven surface, and it is purely a reference for your darkest areas. Wipe over your support with kitchen roll dampened in lighter fuel to remove any particles left by the transtrace, and cover in frisk.

1

2

3

4

5

6
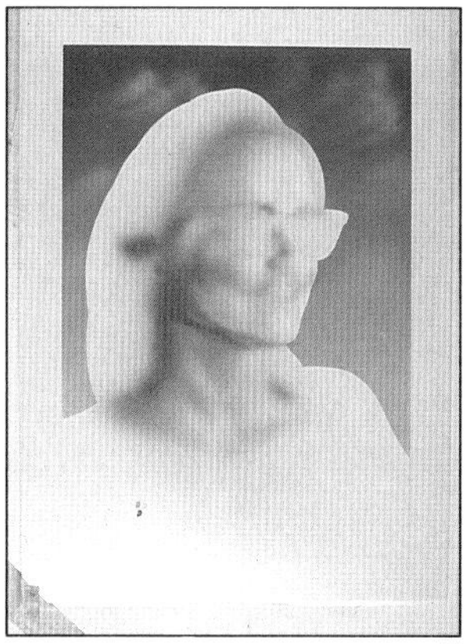

7

3 Cut carefully around the outline of the image with a good, sharp blade, and remove the mask from the background. Sky blue is sprayed, grading down from the top. Remember you are now working in an opaque medium so when your spray hits the surface it will be quite dense. Do not worry if the colour looks solid, and the gradation that you have achieved previously with transparent over-spraying is not apparent. The next stage is to mix in some white with the sky blue, and this time spray from the bottom towards the top. As you have probably gathered by now, you do not have to work from dark to light in an opaque medium, as spraying a lighter shade will cover over the darker areas at the bottom thereby creating a graded tone in reverse.

4 To enhance the background, and add more interest to the overall image, some white clouds were added. With an opaque medium the sky might look a little too solid, so these extra touches are even more important to create the realism. Using opaque white, spray light bursts to suggest the clouds.

5 Remove the remaining mask, and when the paint has dried, lay down a fresh sheet of frisk. Cut the mask carefully so that all the areas of skin are exposed. One of the most difficult parts of spraying skin is achieving the right mix of colours to make it look natural. Although in this case you are going to be told what to use, the secret is to keep testing your mix on a spare sheet of card until it looks correct. You are going to spray the lighter tones first, and for this a mix of white, scarlet lake and yellow ochre (to tone down the pink) proved successful.

6 Now your first pencil drawing will prove invaluable to show you where the darker flesh tones appear. Using your original mix, but with the addition of a little red and red ochre, carefully spray the darker areas freehand. If you are not completely happy with the result, don't worry too much as you can always change back to your lighter mix and tidy things up.

7 Take a sheet of acetate and secure it with low tack masking tape over your original pencil drawing. Make register marks on the acetate with crosses to mark the top corners of the artwork accurately. Cut out the darkest skin areas which have a more linear shape, and the lips.

8 Using your register marks, position the acetate and tape it securely in place. These little marks will prove invaluable as they enable you to move the mask and realign it perfectly over the image. The reason for using acetate with gouache medium is that it enables you to cut the mask away from the surface of the artwork. This is important as your medium is of a much thicker consistency, and you therefore run the risk of cutting through the paint surface when cutting directly over it. Cut out the bottom lip from the underlying frisk and spray in scarlet, following the outer edge close to the surface, and pulling back to fill in the centre, creating a slightly lighter tone. Expose the upper lip and spray

8

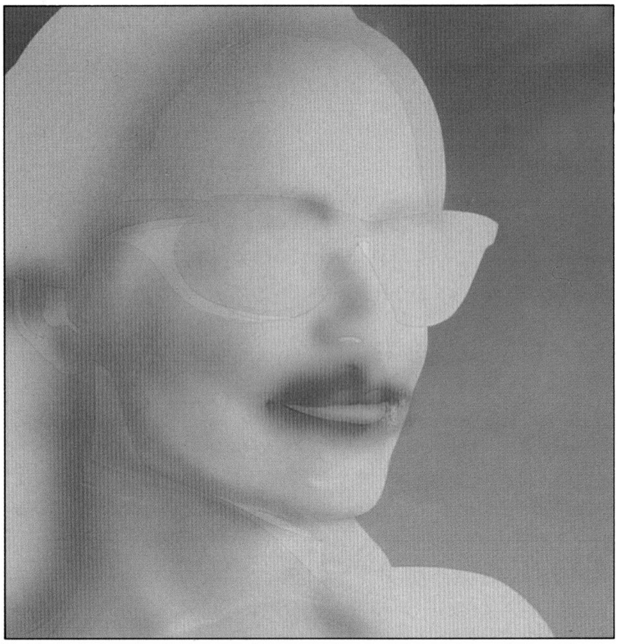

9

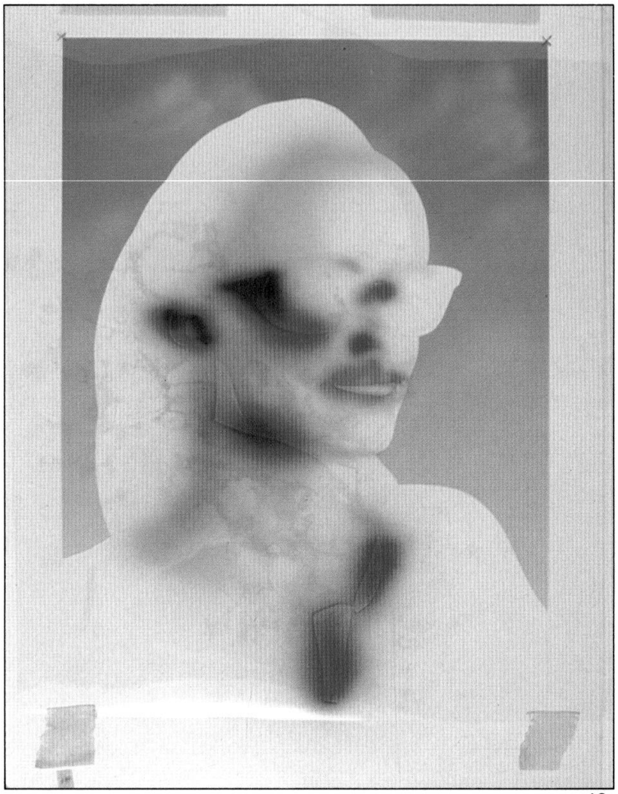

10

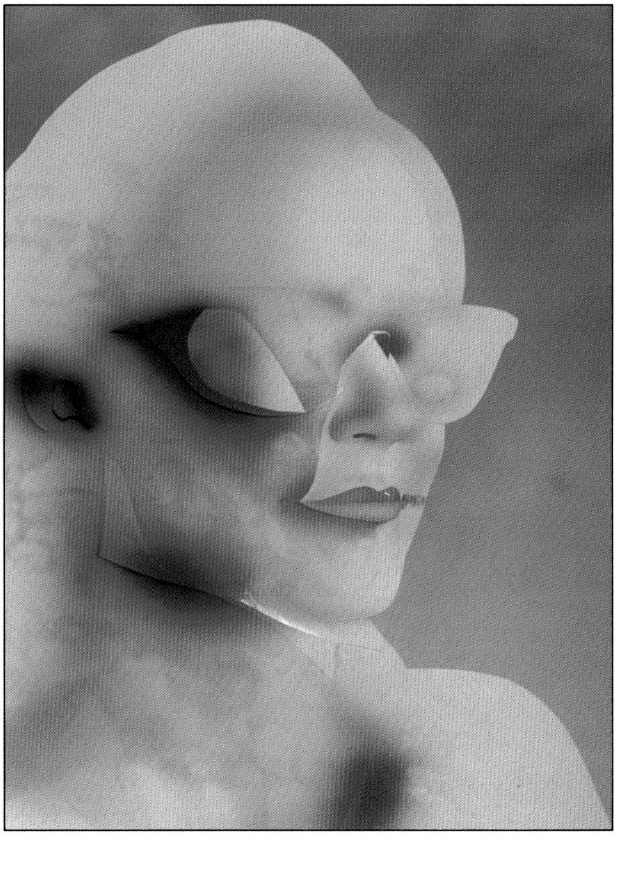

9 With the acetate mask still in place, spray through the areas that you have previously cut for the darker linear skin tones — but not the nose or the area behind the sunglasses. Experiment to create the right mix of paint, but here black, bistre and red ochre were used.

10 Another advantage of acetate is that it does not adhere to the surface. So you can lift it and keep a check on how things are looking as you progress. Do not worry if the skin tones look unnatural and patchy, so long as the dark areas fall in the right places. Following the contour of the nose, spray in the same mix. Then spray the area behind the sunglasses.

11

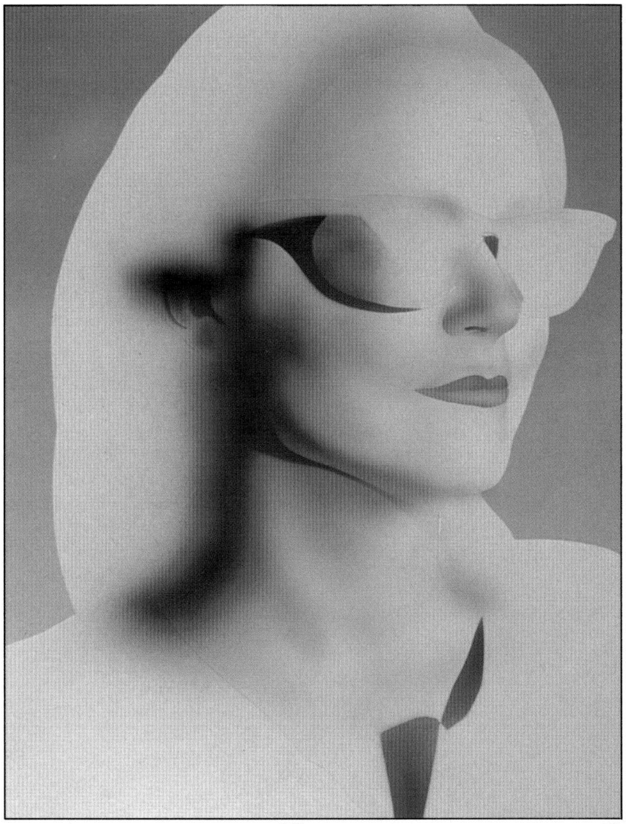

12

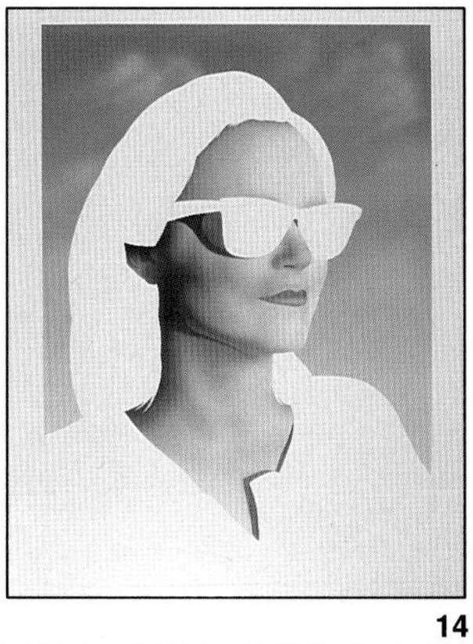

13

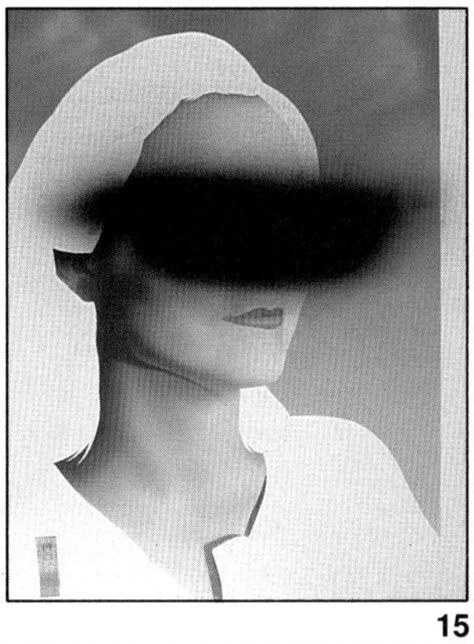

14

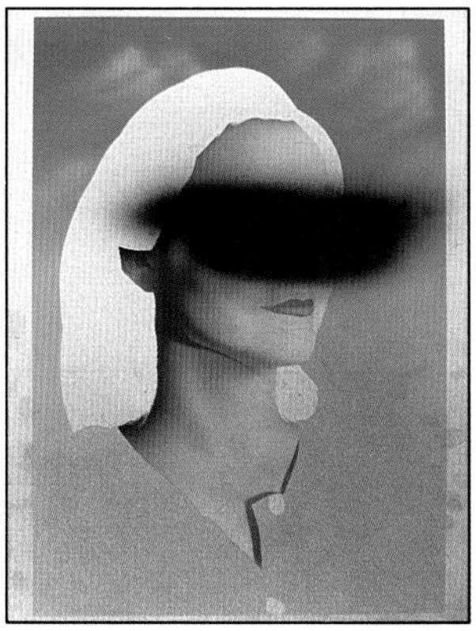

15

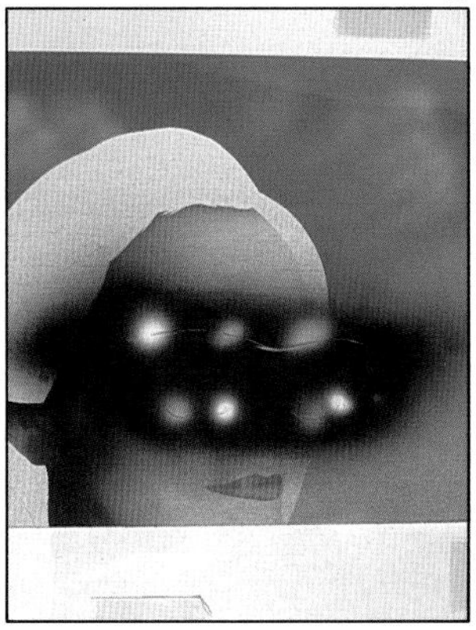

11 Remove the acetate and take a close look. You will notice that you have very defined areas of dark tones, which at this stage seem very out of place and totally unreal. However, this is the difference when working with an opaque medium. Your sprayed patches will look like solid blocks, so they now have to be softened and blended in. Changing back to your original light skin tone, spray over the hard edges freehand to soften and decrease the solid patches, merging them into the rest of the skin.

12 This, so far, has been a gruelling challenge to test your freehand spraying, but as opposed to a transparent medium that will only build on tone, at least mistakes can be more easily corrected with the knowledge that you can over-spray and wipe out! Cover the whole of the image with frisk, and cut the lines for the sunglasses and blouse. Frisk is reintroduced here as the areas that you are going to be working on have not already been sprayed, so there is no chance of damaging the paint's surface.

13 Using your scalpel, carefully peel up the frisk masking the whole of the sunglasses, and expose this area. Cover with a flat, solid spray of black with a hint of indigo added just to take the edge off it. You can get on with another part of the picture while this dries, before you return to carry on with the sunglasses.

14 Now remove the frisk covering the lady's blouse, but make sure that you leave the two buttons covered as you will get back to these later on. Spray over the entire area in black, again mixed with a couple of drops of indigo. Turn the pressure down slightly on your compressor so that you achieve a speckled effect to imitate the texture of a soft material. It could well be worthwhile practising first with different air pressures on a scrap of paper until you find the perfect setting.

15 Once the paint on the blouse has dried, cover the bottom of your artwork with a paper mask to prevent any accidents. Then, using your initial drawing for a guide as before, cut an acetate mask for the minimal highlights around the rims of the glasses, and tape this in place using corner 'x' marks for correct alignment. Spray these areas with permanent white. Since you are working in gouache, this white spray will overcome the heavy black of the sunglasses to create perfect highlights.

16 Take off the acetate, replace it on your drawing and cut out the two lenses. Then further cut out the small triangular area on the right lens where the sky will just show through. Re-align the acetate on your artwork, making sure that the register marks are spot on. Although you have cut out the lenses, place the top three quarters of the right-hand lens down so that only the small 'see-through' bit is exposed. Cover the small rim highlights just below this with 'low tack' tape to prevent any unwanted over-spray, and then spray the 'see through' part in blue with a touch of white to create the illusion of the sky being just barely visible through the glasses. A gentle spray of permanent white can then be added to the top left of the left-hand lens as a small highlight.

17 Again transfer the acetate back to your initial drawing — discarding the remainder of the right-hand lens — and carefully cut out the final small areas of highlighting and the tiny clasp on the side. Carefully reposition it over your artwork and add the merest hint of permanent white to the newly cut out areas, and to the top left of the right-hand lens.

18 Remove the paper mask protecting the bottom of the picture, and reuse it to cover the top of your artwork. Once more using your drawing as a guide, cut an acetate mask for the very darkest parts of the blouse — the bits in dark shadow — and tape it in position over the picture. You can then lay a heavy, flat wash of black and indigo over these areas.

16

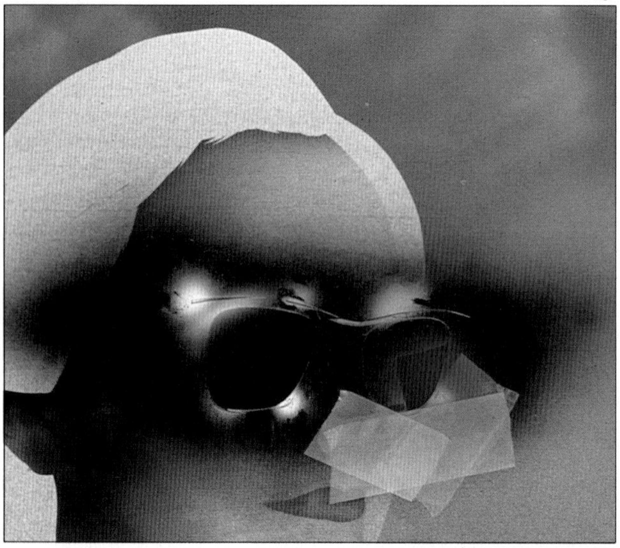

17

18

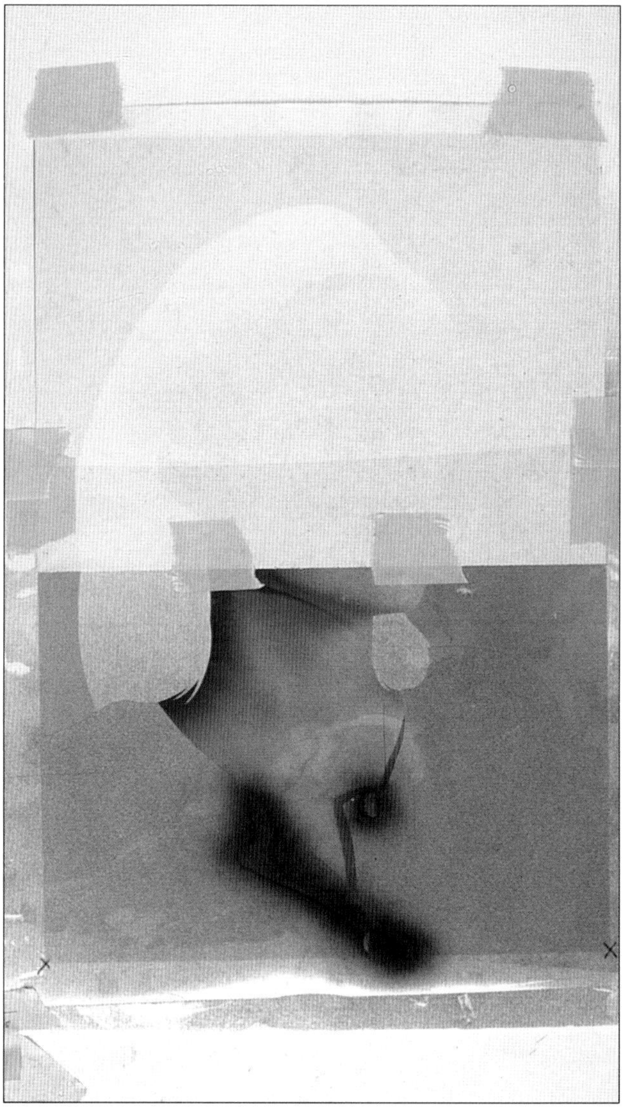

19 Take off the acetate mask to reveal the remainder of the blouse which you have already removed the frisk from when you sprayed the overall speckle effect. Make sure the buttons are still covered, and then spraying freehand add some soft-edged dark areas to the blouse with the usual mix of black and indigo to create gentle folds in the material. Take your time with this, gradually building up the colour for the best results. Allow the blouse to become much darker towards the top where it meets the sky, so that you get a vivid contrast of light and dark which will give your artwork an amazing amount of impact. When you are happy with this area, leave the paint to dry. Once you are totally sure it has, re-mask the whole blouse with frisk, and cut out and expose the buttons. Spray these with a mix of yellow ochre and bistre, sticking to the outlines to create a lighter spot in their middles.

19

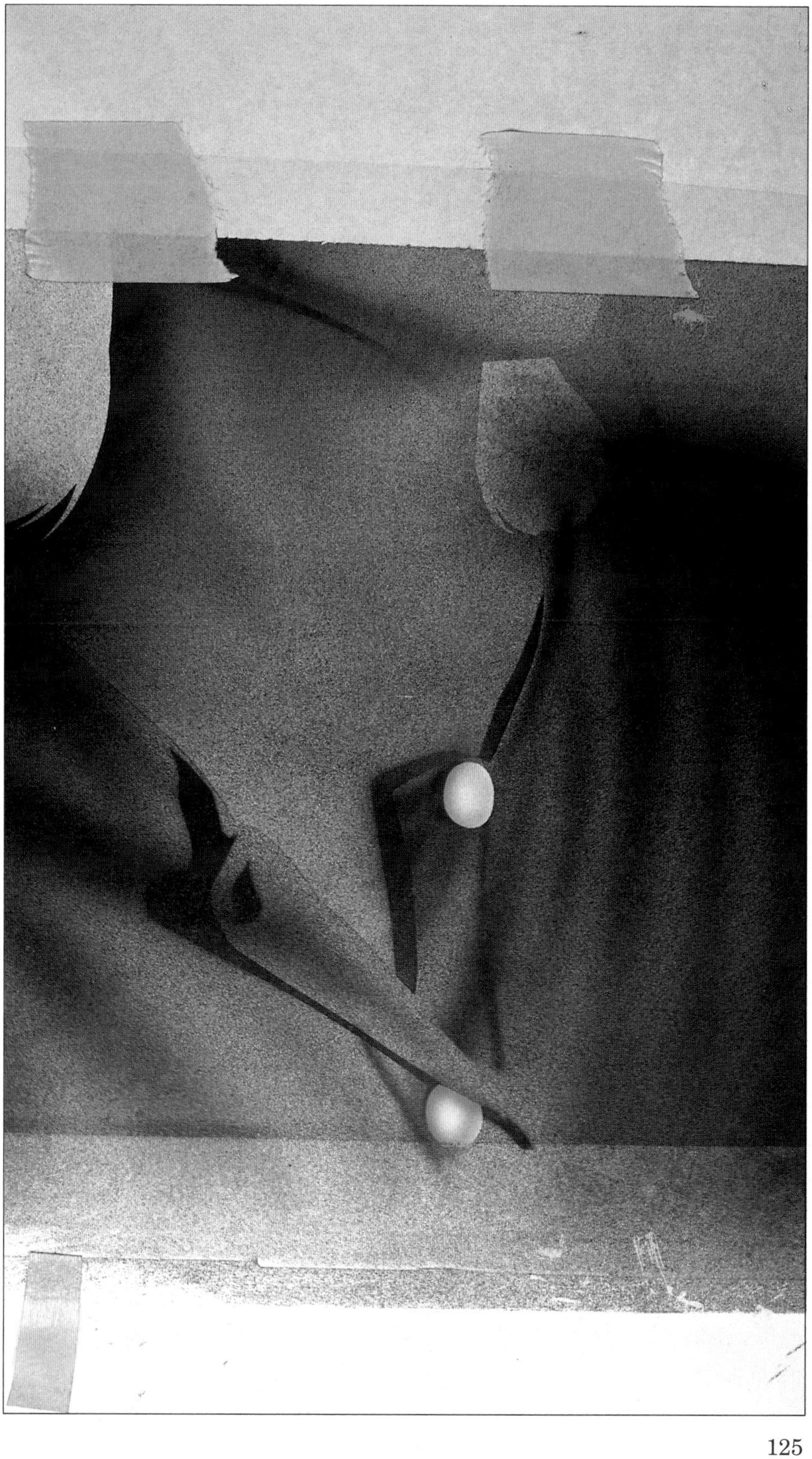

20

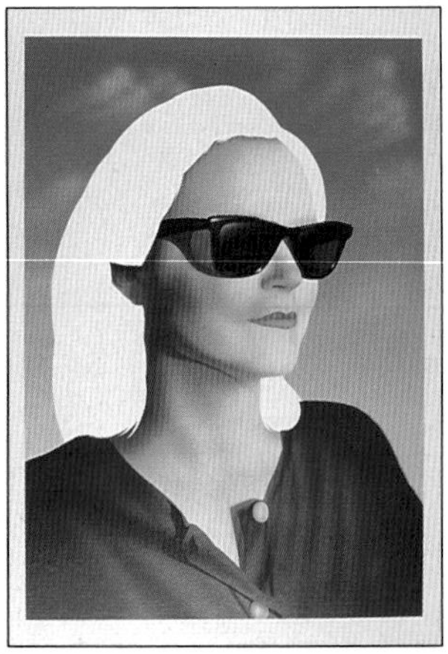

21

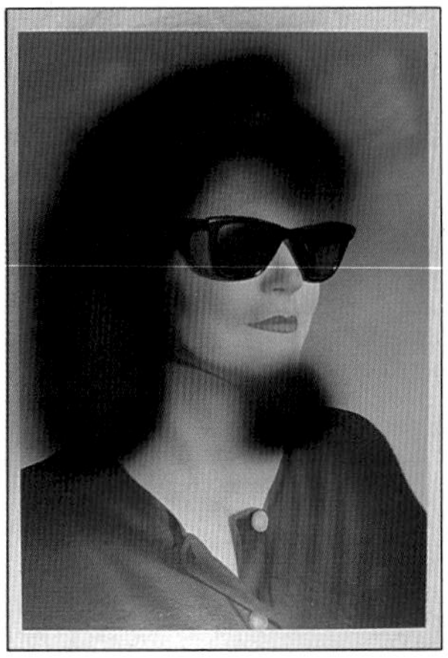

22

23

24

20 Once you are sure that all the sprayed colour is dry, remove any remaining traces of frisk. Lay a fresh sheet of frisk over the entire artwork, using a ruler to make sure that there is no air trapped underneath it. With a fresh scalpel blade, cut very carefully along the outline of the hair.

21 You can now remove the frisk covering all the hair — not forgetting the small piece on the right. Using a mix of black with small amounts of sepia and red ochre, spray a flat colour over these newly exposed sections.

22 Add some tonal variation to the hair with a small amount of sepia sprayed freehand. Then, with the original hair colour mix, paint individual hair strands all over with a sable brush — don't forget to include some loose strands over the ear and onto the face. Although it may seem a waste, it is now time to remove the frisk you have only just laid down so that you can start to add the finishing touches. First are the eyebrows, which are painted on with a sable brush in the same colour as the hair. Then continue by adding detail to the lips in scarlet.

23 The only trouble with gouache — and all opaque mediums — is that you cannot scratch back soft highlights into it successfully, as there is no way of toning these down afterwards. So to create your finishing highlights you will now need to switch exclusively to a sable brush. With a mix of yellow ochre and white carefully paint some highlights into the hair.

24 After hours of hard work you can now at last add the final touches. Using permanent white, include a highlight to the tip of the lady's nose and across her lips. As you can see, this really does finish the artwork off beautifully

Chapter 10

Do your own thing

You have been presented with a range of projects and effects that can be achieved through a mixture of confidence, patience and practice. Some are achieved by simple techniques, others through meticulousness and sheer determination. It is therefore fitting that the final project should show you how all these elements can be combined, and mixed with your own imagination, to create a spectacular piece.

This is the point where you should throw caution to the wind, and do your own thing. Follow the step-by-steps, and use them as a guide and inspiration, not necessarily to follow exactly. Once again have fun. This might not be your style, but what it does give you is the chance to use everything that has been demonstrated in this book. Creative masking, gradating, line control, transparent and opaque media, hard and loose masking — it is all in here. Throughout the whole history of airbrushing new doors have been opened purely through experimentation. Do not be afraid, your ultimate aim is to express yourself, and so by all means enjoy it!

Do your own thing

ABSTRACT

1 On a sheet of detail paper work up your initial layout drawing. Since this is such a complicated image, keep the drawing to outlines only to prevent it from becoming too confused. Do not hesitate to use a ruler and compasses, to make sure that all the circles, stars and so forth are all spot on. The image of the woman's face in the centre was in fact traced from the photograph used in the colour tinting exercise earlier on.

2 Using transtrace paper, transfer this outline image to your support, remembering to wipe over it with lighter fuel to get rid of any 'sootiness'. Cover the support with a sheet of frisk — making sure that there is no air trapped underneath by smoothing it down with a ruler — and then very carefully cut along all the lines for the background areas. All these individual sections are going to be removed one at a time, and a different airbrush effect applied to each. So, moving straight along, start by exposing the top left-hand corner, and spraying a flat wash of yellow gouache all over it.

3 Replace this first mask, and then cut and expose alternate stripes within it. Since this project is such a complicated exercise in masking, make sure that you never completely remove the frisk when revealing an area for spraying, instead just peel it back and fix it out of the way with a piece of tape. This not only allows the masks to be easily replaced, but also prevents you from forgetting which one goes where! Spray over these stripes with red gouache, gradating them from light to dark.

4 Once the paint is dry, carefully replace the mask. You can now move on to the next section at the top right. To this part of the artwork an interesting gridded pattern is to be added, using an old piece of material as a mask. First of all though, just peel back the frisk and spray over with a flat tone of light green gouache.

1

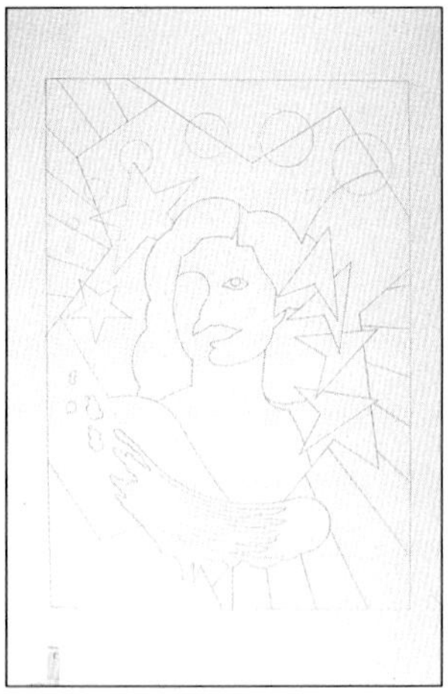

2

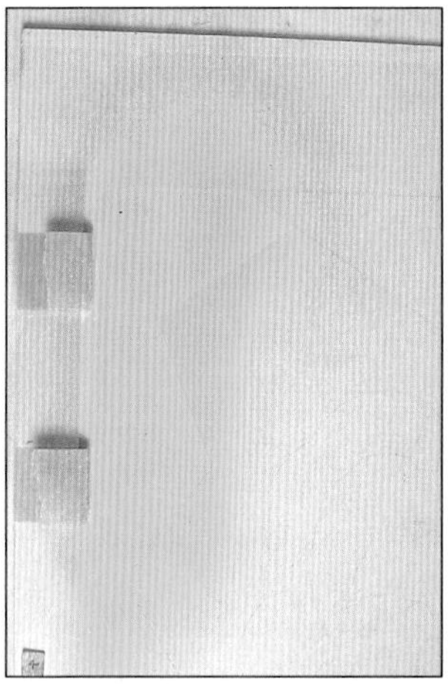

3

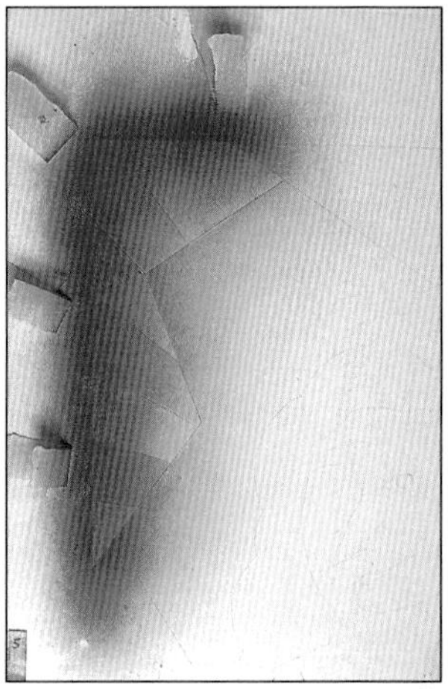

4

5

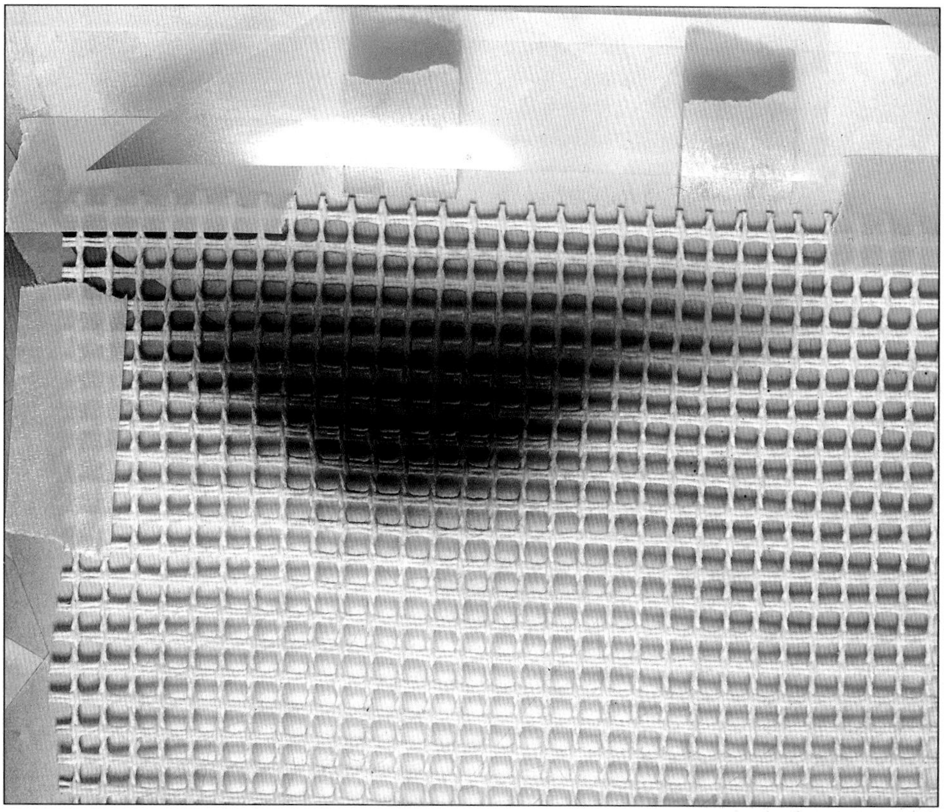

5 Using a piece of heavy, open weave material as a mask, spray over this area again, but this time using a dark green gouache. Do not be tempted into using a piece of netting as it will hardly show up when you spray through it. In fact the material used here is ideal, and was found in a rug-making kit. Once you have sprayed this part and removed the material, you will find that you have a lovely 'crisscross' pattern of light and dark green. When everything is dry, re-cover this part of your picture with its frisk mask.

6

6 The frisk covering the next portion of background is now peeled back and taped out of the way. Spraying gently, lay a base colour of light yellow over the entire area. A blue 'spatter' is then added over the yellow. To get a really good 'spatter' from your airbrush you will need to buy a 'spatter cap' from your local stockist. This is a little device which fits to your airbrush, replacing the nozzle cap, and creates a very granular, textured effect — as you can see here. Practise with this on a scrap of paper first, just to see the different effects you can achieve with the airbrush held at different heights.

7 You can now move on down to the bottom right of the picture, remembering to make sure that the part you have just sprayed is covered first. The frisk in alternate bands of this section is lifted up with the tip of a scalpel, and held back with pieces of tape. Spray these parts with blue, gradating the colour from very dark at the edges, to virtually nothing at the centre of the bands.

8 Replace the frisk, and then expose the unsprayed bands. Gradate these in the same way, this time using Bordeaux red. When laying down a gradated tone, never restrict your strokes to just the area to be sprayed. The effect will always look far better if you continue past each end and onto the mask, so that you do not get a build up of colour.

9 The area below, and to the left of the woman's face is now uncovered. Take care to leave the frisk masking the blobs trailing behind the 'paint streak' in place, since you will get to these later on. Using a green gouache, do some freehand spraying of blotches over the exposed area. Then switch to red ochre, and again spraying freehand, add some faint swirly trails wherever you fancy.

10 Pause for a bit while all this paint dries, and then carefully replace the frisk, making sure that all the edges line up. For the next area, the very bottom left, you are going to create the effect of wood. So first of all peel back the frisk mask from it, and then spray all over it with the base colour of yellow ochre with a few drops of white added.

7

8

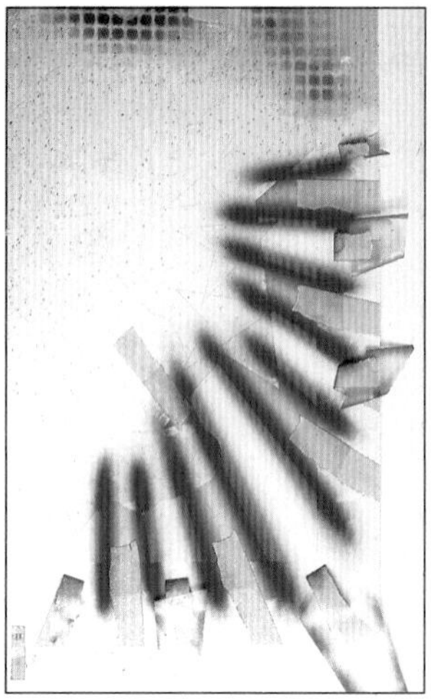

9

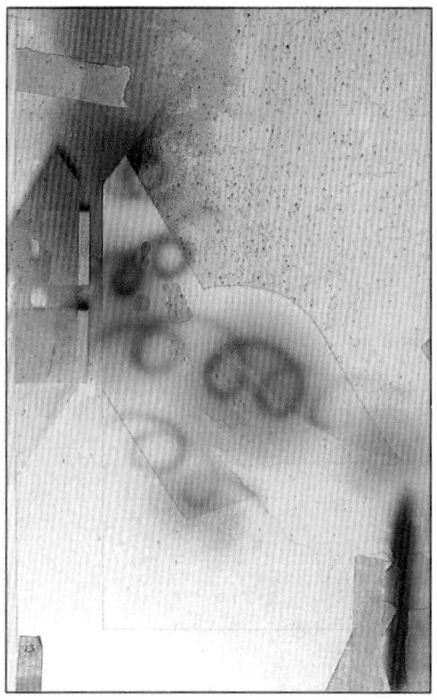

10

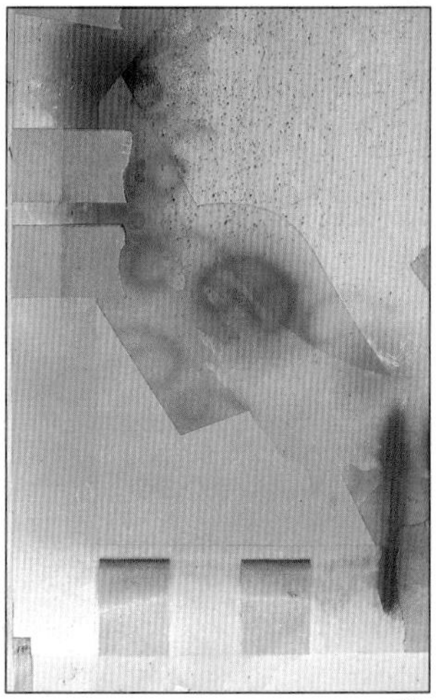

11 On a sheet of paper, roughly draw some lines to imitate the 'grain' in a piece of wood. Cut the middle section out, and then place this down over the exposed piece of your artwork. Following the edges of the paper, spray a tone of Venetian red — dark to the left and very light on the right. Repeat this process, removing a section at a time and spraying along the edges, to gradually build up the 'wood grain' on your artwork. As you are using a loose paper mask, the lines in the 'grain', although noticeable, will not be so strong as to make the 'wood' appear disjointed and unrealistic. If on finishing the 'wood' you feel that you have been a bit too heavy with the Venetian red, remember that you are working in gouache. It is always possible to switch back to the base colour of yellow ochre and white, and then very gently spray over any spoilt areas to 'knock back' the red.

11

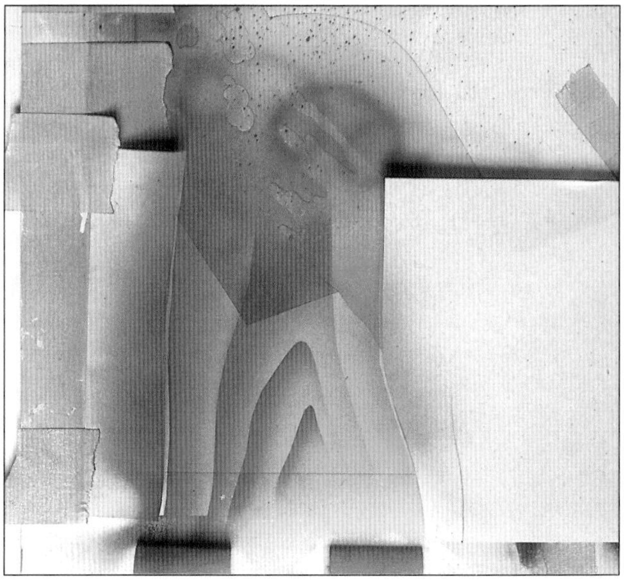

12 Recover the entire area, and then move on to the left side of the woman's hair. Tape the frisk masking out of the way, and then, with the airbrush held slightly back from the support, spray along the right-hand edge in Venetian red gouache. As you can see this gives a very deep colour down one side, with a sudden change to only a hint of colour just a step out from it.

13 Ensuring the paint has dried move straight along, exposing the two sections of background to the right of the woman's face. The 'ripple' effect is created by spraying freehand in sky blue. Starting at the top, with your airbrush close to the support, spray continual sweeps towards the bottom, gradually increasing the height of your airbrush and the width of the sweeps as you go. Do not forget to continue down with your sweeps onto the second smaller area.

12

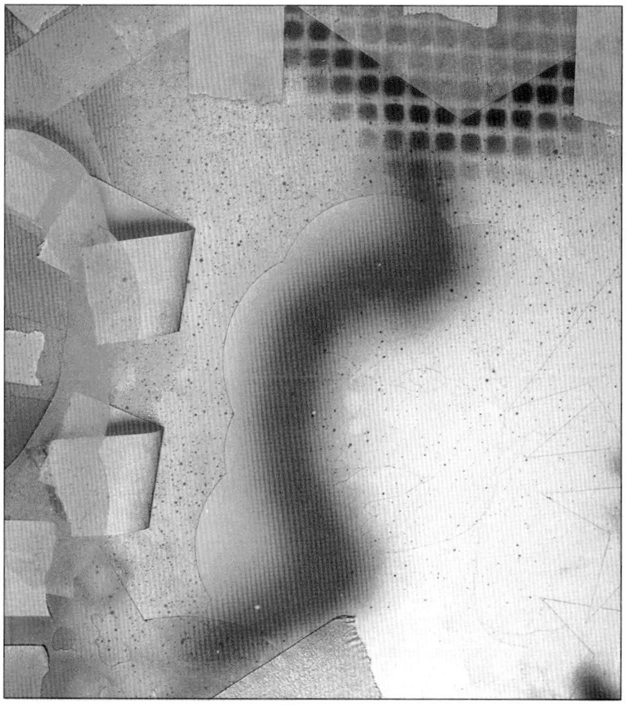

13

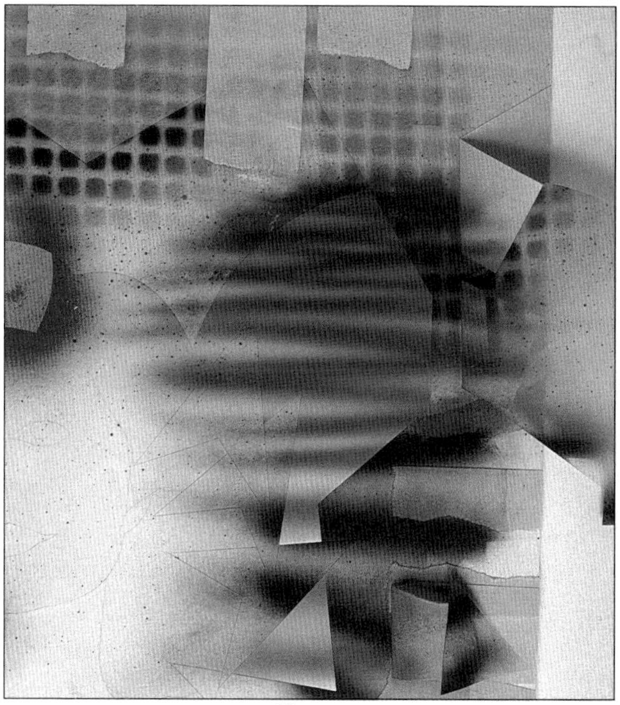

14

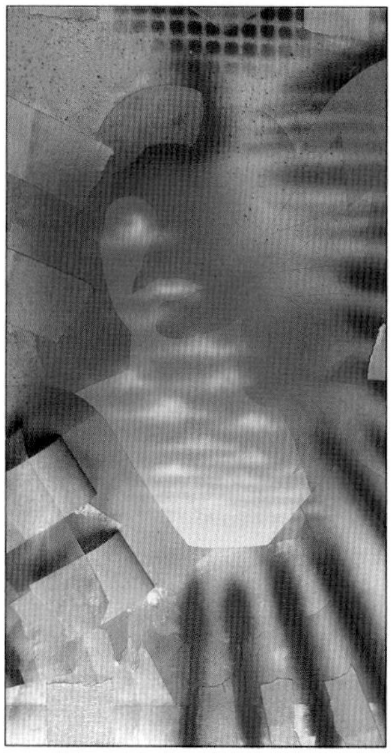

14 Fold back the masking covering the neck of the woman and the left-hand side of her face, and spray a gradated tone from top to bottom of sky blue gouache. Allow this to dry, and then add some clouds by spraying freehand in opaque white. If you are feeling really confident with your airbrush control, a really nice touch is to add a small cloud to imitate the woman's left eye, and a flat, spindly cloud for the middle of her lips.

15

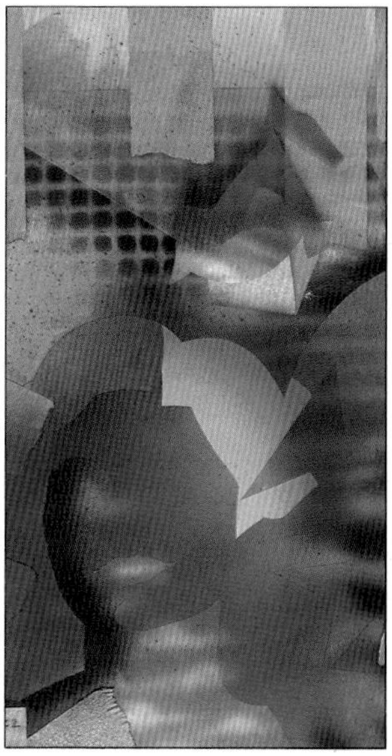

15 Moving on to the next area, the right of the woman's hair, peel back the frisk to expose it, and spray all over with a very gentle wash of a red and white mixture. Continue with the area, by overspraying in an opaque bright green, gradating this lighter towards the centre of the artwork. Remember, as with each stage of this project, to allow the paint to dry and replace the frisk before continuing.

16 You can now remove the frisk to expose the bottom right of the woman's hair, although make sure that you do not take it completely away — as before just hold it to one side with a piece of tape. Spray a base coat of yellow, mixed with white, all over this area. Then try flicking drops of red paint onto the support with a brush. Do not worry about how well this works, as this is an abstract piece of work, nobody will realise what effect you were attempting to achieve! Finish this area off by adding a few soft spots of yellow ochre sprayed freehand.

17 The stripes just below the last section are next on the list. Since each alternate stripe has its own tiny mask, taping these back would be fiddly. Just remove them completely from your artwork. Spray over the area with a flat wash of red gouache. Once the paint has dried, do not replace all the bits of frisk individually as there is very little chance that you would get them all to fit. It is much easier to cover the part with a few strips of clear low tack tape.

18 Using a couple of bits of tape as a 'hinge', fold back the frisk covering the right half of the woman's face. Fill this section in with a solid spray of black gouache. Your 'spatter cap' can once again show its worth, by being used to add an opaque white gouache 'spatter' over the area for the effect of stars in a night sky. This is further enhanced by spraying with your normal nozzle, a white spot on top of a few of the 'stars', holding the airbrush very close to the support to get them as small as possible. Fold the frisk forward for a moment, note where the woman's pupil should be, and also create a soft dot here.

19 As a finishing touch to this 'night sky' a couple of 'starbursts' can now be added. Although this may sound difficult, it is in fact a very simple technique which gives amazing results. Cut a large cross in a square of frisk, place this over one of your worked up 'stars', and then spray a burst of white at its centre.

16

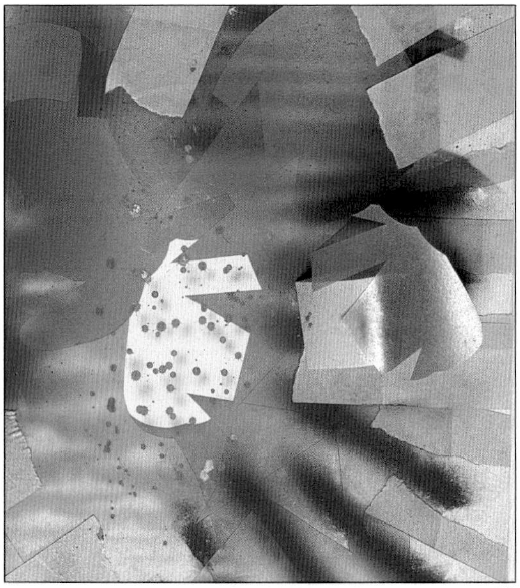

17

18

19

20 When you take off the frisk you will find a lovely 'starburst', and as long as you cut the cross quite big, its arms should taper off to nothing. Only add a couple of these, but do make sure that one is included where the woman's pupil will be. To then finish off these 'starbursts', spray freehand at their centres to diffuse the intensity slightly.

21 Up until now you have been working in gouache, but for the remainder of this work, watercolour is to be used. With the incredibly high number of masks used so far, your artwork could well be looking a real mess. So this is a good chance to remove all the various pieces of frisk and tape. Once you have got everything off, re-cover the entire work with a sheet of detail paper, and cut out windows over the two remaining unsprayed areas — the 'paint streak' and the arrow heads. Next, lay frisk on these sections, and cut along all the remaining lines.

22 First to be tackled is the 'paint streak'. Using a piece of tape, hinge the first section to be sprayed out of the way, and spray along the bottoms of the 'paint trails' with a mix of crimson and ultramarine watercolours. Once this is dry fold the frisk back into place.

20

21

22

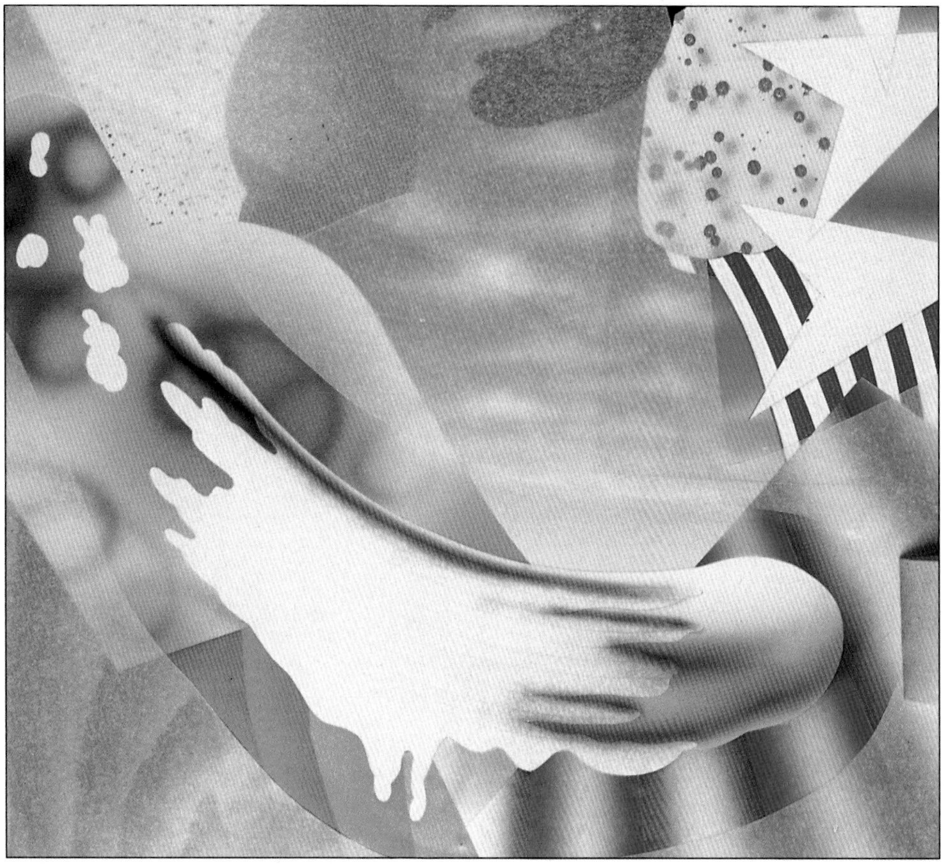

23

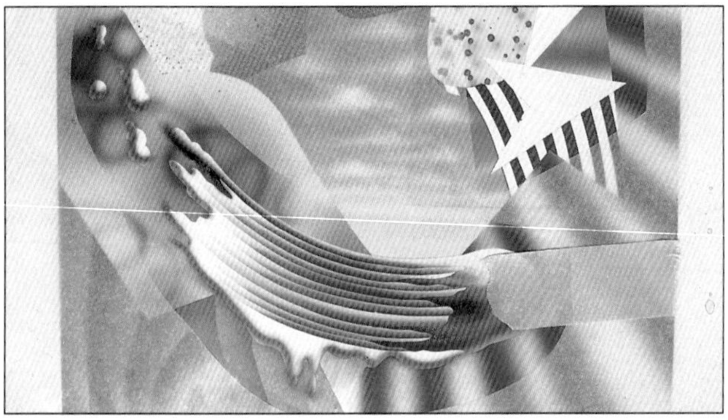

24

23 The next mask down can be totally removed, and the same colour mix added along the bottom of the strip. This process is repeated with each individual mask in turn, always spraying along the bottom edge. The number of masks you use depends on how detailed you want your 'paint streak' to be. In this case there are five individual sections, not forgetting the few loose blobs trailing along behind.

24 Although this is now really starting to look like a good 'paint streak', it can be finished off by removing the initial mask completely, and over-spraying the entire area — including the blobs — with a watercolour scarlet. You have finished with this part of the picture for the moment, so for a bit of protection, cover it with a paper mask.

25

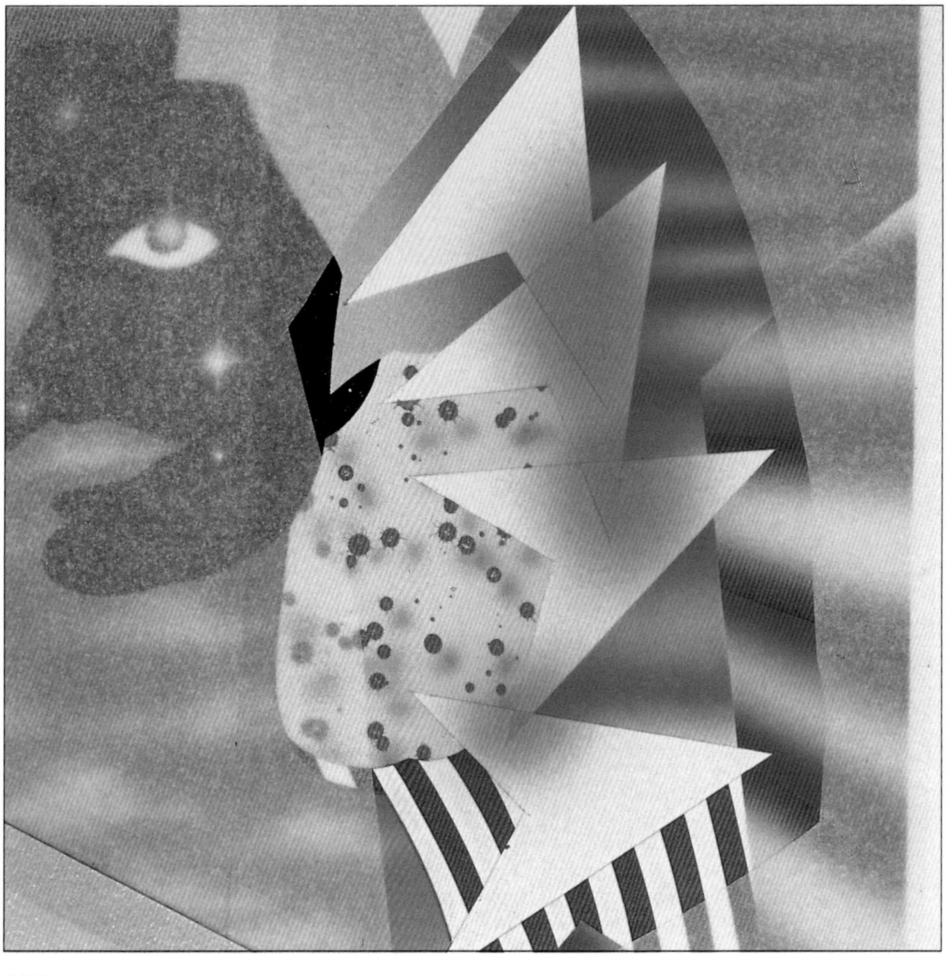

25 It is now time to tackle the last remaining area of support left uncovered. As you have switched to watercolours, the arrow heads can be easily made to appear transparent by the use of over-spraying. The frisk covering the very darkest parts — where they overlap — is removed and sprayed with a light blue.

26 The frisk covering each arrow head is hinged out of the way in turn, and the area sprayed with light blue. Once one is finished, replace its mask, and move on to the next. Because you have already sprayed the overlapping parts once, and will over-spray them twice more as you work through the arrow heads, they will appear much darker. On the other hand, since you are replacing the masks for the tops of the arrow heads as you go, these will be sprayed once only, and so will be much lighter. The combination of these light and dark areas together creates the effect of the arrow heads being almost transparent.

27 Remove all the masking on your artwork, and re-cover it with a fresh sheet of frisk. Then, working round the picture, cut the masks for the various drop shadows. Starting at the top left, add a small red shadow to the top of the red and yellow banded section, and then continue with grey shadows lying on top of the large blue speckled area.

28 Next on the list of shadows are those on the woman's hair — red on one side and a very dark grey on the other. Both of these use a mask which is cut straight along the edge of the hair, but allowed to step in on the inside, and the area is then sprayed closely following the 'hard' outside line. A very solid drop shadow can then be included under the topmost of the arrow heads. This is simply a small mask which is cut out and sprayed with a solid grey watercolour.

29 The soft shadow on top of the wood is achieved by exposing the whole of the wood area, and then spraying with Venetian red watercolour, closely along its top border. By selecting the same colour that was used for the 'grain' in the wood, this shadow will merge in and look very realistic. Next, remove the frisk from the area under the 'paint streak' and add a freehand sprayed soft shadow. Lay the colour slowly and gradually build up the tone.

26

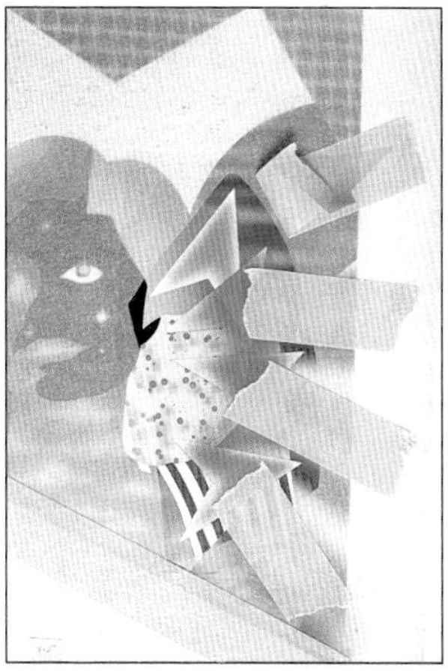

27

28

29

30

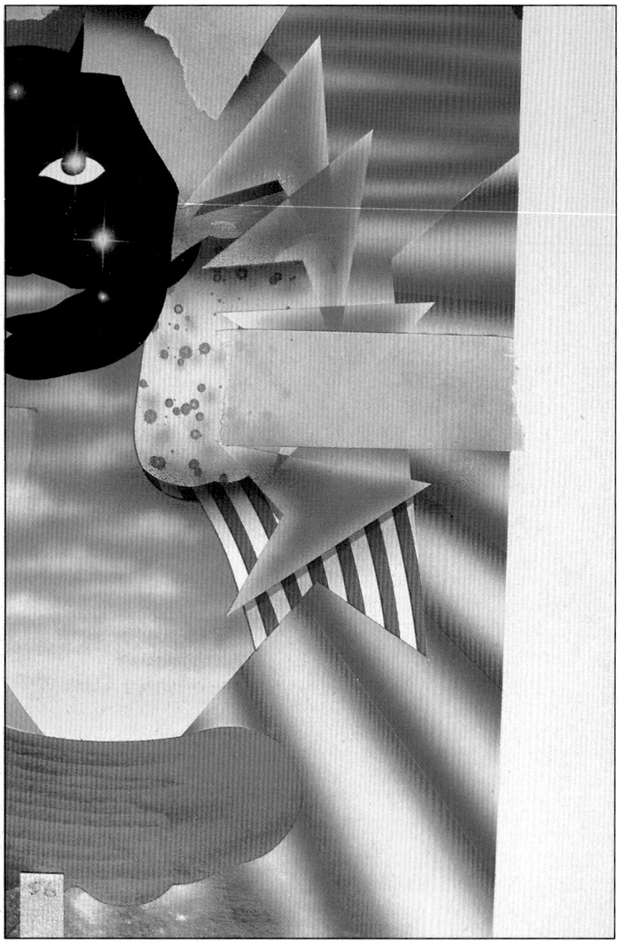

30 The final shadows can at last be included. Give the remaining arrow heads either a solid drop shadow with a set-size mask, or a softer shadow by exposing more of your artwork and spraying close to the edge. It is also worthwhile to note the different depths given to the various shadows throughout the picture, so that a complete scale of heights is achieved. Last, but by no means least, a soft shadow under the spotty effect can be gently sprayed.

31 Do not despair, because you are nearly there! Remove all the frisk from your artwork, and cover the bottom half with a paper mask. Then using the direct image transfer method, pick up the circles from your initial drawing onto a piece of frisk, and place this down over the top of your picture. With a very sharp scalpel cut along the circles' outlines. Each of these can be removed in turn, and sprayed not only in different colours, but in different ways. Some can be solid, some outline only.

31

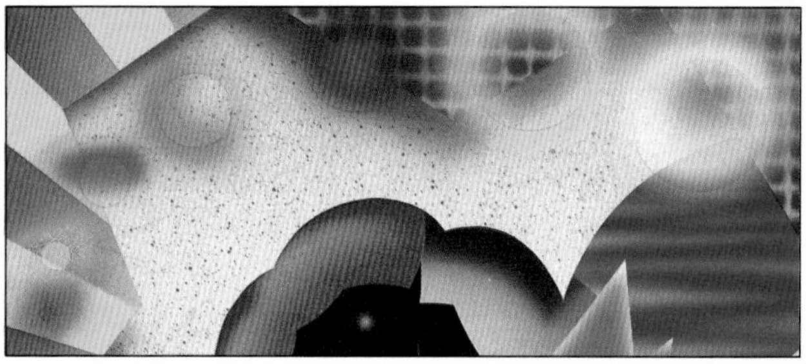

32

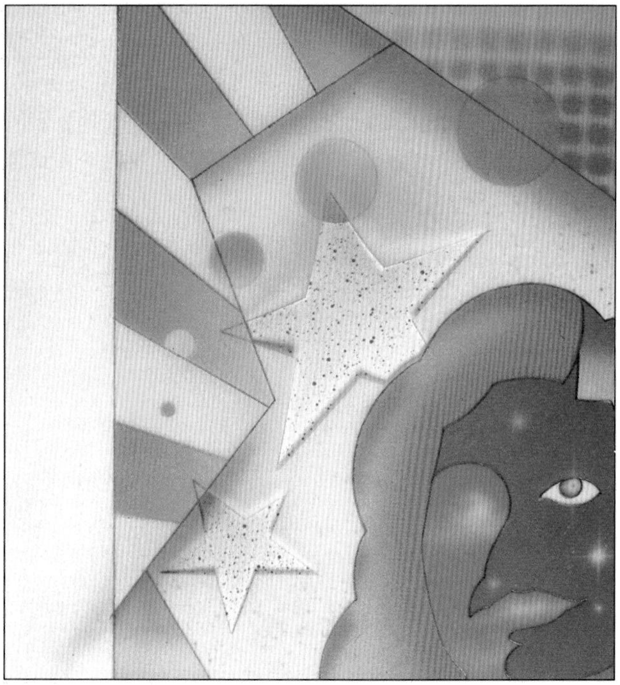

32 As this is the final stage, it is now safe to use your initial drawing as a mask itself. Cut out the two stars, and place this down over your artwork. Then spray a light gradated tone of sky blue from top to bottom within each one. Obviously, if you really want to keep your initial drawing for prosperity you can again use the direct image transfer method to copy the stars across. However you choose to approach this last step, when you lift up your mask, you will expose your finished masterpiece to the world — but warn them first, for they could well need sunglasses!

Index